180 Bible Verses for a

LESS STRESSED LIFE

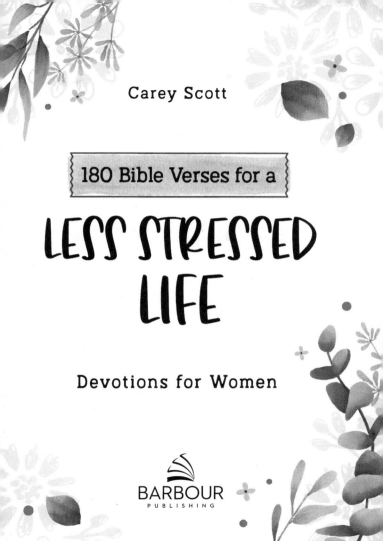

Carey Scott

180 Bible Verses for a

LESS STRESSED LIFE

Devotions for Women

BARBOUR
PUBLISHING

Scripture quotations marked MSG are taken from *THE MESSAGE*, copyright © 1993, 2002, 2018 by Eugene H. Peterson. Used by permission of NavPress. All rights reserved. Represented by Tyndale House Publishers, Inc.

Scripture quotations marked AMPC are taken from the Amplified® Bible, Copyright © 1954, 1958, 1962, 1964, 1965, 1987 by The Lockman Foundation. Used by permission.

Scripture quotations marked AMP are taken from the Amplified® Bible, Copyright © 2015 by The Lockman Foundation. Used by permission.

Scripture quotations marked CEB are taken from the Common English Bible® Copyright © 2010, 2011 by Common English Bible.™ Used by permission.

Scripture quotations marked TPT are from The Passion Translation®. Copyright © 2017, 2018, 2020 by Passion & Fire Ministries, Inc. Used by permission. All rights reserved. ThePassionTranslation.com.

Scripture quotations marked VOICE are taken from The Voice™. Copyright © 2008 by Ecclesia Bible Society. Used by permission. All rights reserved.

Published by Barbour Publishing, Inc., 1810 Barbour Drive, Uhrichsville, Ohio 44683, www.barbourbooks.com

Our mission is to inspire the world with the life-changing message of the Bible.

Printed in the United States of America.

If you want to live a less stressed life, it will require God's help. We simply cannot do it on our own because life is full of people and circumstances that cause us to worry. From challenging relationships to tight finances to the state of the world, there are ample opportunities for fear. And anxiety not only keeps us stirred up during the day, but it also negatively impacts a good night's sleep. The truth is if we look to anyone or anything other than God to settle our restless heart, we'll be disappointed. Let this book encourage you to invite God into the stress so He can exchange it for the peace you're desperate to find. Meditate on the scriptures reminding you that you're not alone. And learn to trust the Lord to be your source for help and hope no matter what you're facing. He's ready and waiting.

Untangling Worry and Stress

*Don't fret or worry. Instead of worrying, pray.
Let petitions and praises shape your worries into
prayers, letting God know your concerns. Before
you know it, a sense of God's wholeness, everything
coming together for good, will come and settle
you down. It's wonderful what happens when
Christ displaces worry at the center of your life.*

PHILIPPIANS 4:6–7 MSG

You may be thinking you have no hope of walking out today's verse. Maybe worry and stress are constant companions in your life. They are familiar feelings. Maybe your family has a long history of passing them down through the generations. But don't underestimate the power of prayer to untangle them. When you choose to take stress and worry to the Lord the moment they begin to knot you up, scripture says doing so will settle your spirit. His presence will bring a peace over your tangled heart, and you will be free.

Being Content with Who You Are

So be content with who you are, and don't put on airs. God's strong hand is on you; he'll promote you at the right time. Live carefree before God; he is most careful with you.

1 PETER 5:6-7 MSG

Few things are harder for women than being content with ourselves. We have such a critical eye, comparing and judging who we are against those we decide are better. The result is a state of constant stress that makes us second guess our value on the regular. God's desire is for us to live carefree, but at times that feels impossible. How can we relax when we're constantly stressed out? Remember: God made you on purpose. He thought up everything about you, and He delights in His creation! Ask the Lord to help you find contentment and acceptance, and ask Him to remove any expectations of perfection.

God's Perfect Peace

*"I leave the gift of peace with you—my peace.
Not the kind of fragile peace given by the world,
but my perfect peace. Don't yield to fear or be
troubled in your hearts—instead, be courageous!"*

JOHN 14:27 TPT

There is a big difference between the kind of peace the world offers and the peace that comes from trusting in the Lord. The former is fragile and easily shattered. It's unstable and unpredictable. With the smallest challenge, it will fail and leave you feeling hopeless. But God's peace is perfect. It will hold up under the weight of worry every time. It will weather the storm of stress no matter what. So the next time you're feeling overwhelmed by what this life brings, go right to the Lord in prayer. Rather than grab on to the counterfeit calm of the world, let God's peace wash over you instead. It's the real deal.

Never Be Worried

"This is why I tell you to never be worried about your life, for all that you need will be provided, such as food, water, clothing—everything your body needs. Isn't there more to your life than a meal? Isn't your body more than clothing?"

MATTHEW 6:25 TPT

The Lord makes a bold promise in today's verse by saying that He will provide everything you need. That means you can take in a deep breath of peace and exhale the stress that's held you in bondage. It's not up to you. You don't have to be the one to figure it all out. In God's unmatched love for you, He has already made a way. Your needs are top of mind, and His expectations don't include you stressing out over the details. The Lord says to *never* be worried because *all* will be provided. Your job is to trust Him.

You Are More Important

*Look at the birds in the sky. They do not store
food for winter. They don't plant gardens.
They do not sow or reap—and yet, they are
always fed because your heavenly Father
feeds them. And you are even more precious
to Him than a beautiful bird. If He looks after
them, of course He will look after you.*

MATTHEW 6:26 VOICE

If God takes care of the birds, you can rest knowing
He will also take care of you. He loves the birds—He
created them! But you are more important, according
to scripture. You are His prized creation! So what keeps
you from grabbing on to this truth? Why do you doubt
His love for you? Why are you drowning in depression
when you should be trusting in faith? Nothing will stop
His love and care from overwhelming you in the best of
ways. Always expect His goodness to prevail.

Feasting on Worry

*"And who of you by worrying can add
one hour to [the length of] his life?"*
MATTHEW 6:27 AMP

What are you worried about right now? What keeps you stirred up and fearful? Maybe you're struggling to get pregnant or are stressed as you wait to hear from the adoption agency. You may be overwhelmed as a single mom and worried about your ability to keep going. Maybe you're anxious about your marriage or are wondering if you'll ever find a husband. Are you facing a health challenge? Is your stress from financial strain? Life offers a menu of things to worry about, and too often we choose to feast on them. Talk about a recipe for instability that adds nothing to the mix except pain. Instead, why not invite God to the table and let Him bring peace and perspective in a way only He can?

Abandon Your Worries

"So then, forsake your worries! Why would you say, 'What will we eat?' or 'What will we drink?' or 'What will we wear?' For that is what the unbelievers chase after. Doesn't your heavenly Father already know the things your bodies require?"

MATTHEW 6:31-32 TPT

It's time to abandon your worries. Walk away from the stress. Reject the fear that keeps you up at night. Quit entertaining what overwhelms you. Leave behind every bit of anxiety and tension. You don't have to fix your life! You aren't the one to make the puzzle pieces fit together! When you decide you are God, it's a setup to fail. Instead, trust that the Lord has full and complete knowledge of everything you need. He sees it all. He knows your emotional needs. He understands your financial situation. God recognizes the tangible necessities that occupy your mind every day. Trust Him.

Refusing to Worry about Tomorrow

*"So above all, constantly seek God's kingdom
and his righteousness, then all these less
important things will be given to you abundantly.
Refuse to worry about tomorrow, but deal with
each challenge that comes your way, one day
at a time. Tomorrow will take care of itself."*
MATTHEW 6:33-34 TPT

Tomorrow has a way of stirring up all sorts of stress, doesn't it? The problem is that, in our state of worry, we often predict horrible outcomes and endings that do little to settle us down. We imagine everything that could go wrong, and we solidify it in our minds. We decide it's truth. So we let ourselves stress out about ideas that aren't even a sure thing. God wants you to refuse worrying about tomorrow. He wants you to focus on the here and now, taking one day at a time and trusting Him with it all.

Bow Down and Surrender

So bow down under God's strong hand;
then when the time comes, God will lift
you up. Since God cares for you, let Him
carry all your burdens and worries.

1 PETER 5:6–7 VOICE

When scripture tells us to bow down, it means we surrender to the Lord. We take a knee as we give up control over our lives and our circumstances. It's telling Him we're unable to handle the weight of worry and need His help. It's admitting we're not God as we recognize our position in relation to His. Believe that the Lord is deeply invested in you. He cares about every detail of your life. When you're feeling overwhelmed by burdens too heavy to carry, let your next move be to bow down and set them at His feet. Give your worries to God, and He will lift you up.

Empowered for All Things

I have strength for all things in Christ Who empowers me [I am ready for anything and equal to anything through Him Who infuses inner strength into me; I am self-sufficient in Christ's sufficiency].

PHILIPPIANS 4:13 AMPC

In our own ability, we are mighty for only a moment. We have juice for only a jiffy. Our strength is short-lived, and it inevitably produces stress and frustration. Thanks to our human condition, we have limitations that keep us grounded and reliant on God. He designed it this way. And because He made us to be in community with Him and in need of a Savior, we will fall short every time without God's infusion. But the good news is that with His strength, we are empowered to do all things. In His love and compassion, God adds His *super* to our *natural*, giving us abilities we alone don't have.

Fear Is Not from God

For God did not give us a spirit of timidity or cowardice or fear, but [He has given us a spirit] of power and of love and of sound judgment and personal discipline [abilities that result in a calm, well-balanced mind and self-control].

2 TIMOTHY 1:7 AMP

In those moments when you feel fear and stress, know they are not from God. When you're worried and your thoughts are filled with anxiety, He isn't the source. Quite the opposite, actually. God's Word is clear when it confirms that through the Spirit we receive power, love, discipline, and sound judgment from our Father. That means we are capable of self-control. We can have a well-balanced mind. And rather than be stressed out and frazzled, we can experience a sense of calm that will quiet every fear. Ask the Lord for help embracing it.

It's a Command

"I've commanded you to be brave and strong, haven't I? Don't be alarmed or terrified, because the LORD your God is with you wherever you go."

JOSHUA 1:9 CEB

It's important to recognize that when God told Joshua to be brave and strong, it was a *command*. And friend, this directive is for us to live out too. It's not a suggestion for us to ponder. It's not an idea for us to float around. It's not a hope or desire God is crossing His holy fingers for. Instead, it's a bold statement that demands our attention. So the next time your life feels overwhelming or things feel out of control, and anxiety begins to take over, remember His command and straighten your back. Lift your chin. Know that God is always with you. No matter the battle, He is there to give you courage and confidence to keep the weight of worry off your shoulders.

The Temptation to Want More

Don't be obsessed with getting more material things. Be relaxed with what you have. Since God assured us, "I'll never let you down, never walk off and leave you," we can boldly quote, God is there, ready to help; I'm fearless no matter what. Who or what can get to me?

HEBREWS 13:5-6 MSG

The temptation to want more is real. It's stressful! The harsh reality is that it's often hard to feel satisfied when everyone around us is obsessed with the latest and greatest. There's something inside that makes us want to keep up so we can fit in. We want to feel relevant and significant. We want to feel accepted, like we belong. And sometimes piling up material goodies does that. But God is offering you His constant presence. He will fill the empty space that makes you feel unimportant, and He will remove the stress that triggers insecurities.

Leaving Them at His Feet

*So here's what I've learned through it all: Leave
all your cares and anxieties at the feet of the
Lord, and measureless grace will strengthen you.*

PSALM 55:22 TPT

Stress makes us feel weak because we're doing everything we can to keep ourselves together. All our energy is focused on managing fear and worry, leaving us vulnerable in every other area of life. In our exhaustion, we often take out those cares and anxieties on the ones we care about the most. Our personal relationships suffer. Our marriage is put on the back burner. Our kids suffer, confused by our quick-to-anger attitude. But we have a heavenly Father who invites us to lean on Him when we're battling seasons of stress. We can off-load each worry at His feet, exchanging them for strength to navigate the challenging times and remain compassionate toward our loved ones.

He Isn't Hiding

*God, listen to my prayer! Don't hide your heart
from me when I cry out to you! Come close
to me and give me your answer. Here I am,
moaning and restless. I'm preoccupied with
the threats of my enemies and crushed by the
pressure of their opposition. They surround
me with trouble and terror. In their fury they
rise up against me in an angry uproar.*

PSALM 55:1-3 TPT

Sometimes in our stress, we think God isn't interested. He feels far away, so we assume He's too busy. When He doesn't answer quickly, we get anxious, wondering if He's going to come through at all. We end up restless and stressed out, hyperfocused on everything but God. These are the times when we need to cling to His promises the most. This is when we need to remember that, while it may feel He is far away and uninterested, it simply isn't true.

Rely on Him Completely

Place your trust in the Eternal; rely on Him completely; never depend upon your own ideas and inventions. Give Him the credit for everything you accomplish, and He will smooth out and straighten the road that lies ahead.

PROVERBS 3:5-6 VOICE

The safest place to be when you're feeling overwhelmed by life is in God's presence. While we can see only a sliver of the situation, He is able to see it in its entirety. The Lord knows why it's stressing you out. He understands the triggers that stirred up your emotions. God gets the reasons why you are worried and scared. So trying to save yourself seems silly because you are lacking critical details. You simply don't have all the information. Friend, take today's scripture to heart and put your trust in God alone. He will not only straighten your path but also calm your anxious heart.

He Knows Your Future

*For I know the thoughts and plans that I
have for you, says the Lord, thoughts and
plans for welfare and peace and not for evil,
to give you hope in your final outcome.*
JEREMIAH 29:11 AMPC

It's easy to become worried about our future, especially when our best laid plans aren't working out as we'd hoped. Maybe you're still single or still not pregnant. Maybe you haven't yet carved out time to go back to school and finish your degree. Maybe you're facing divorce or bankruptcy once again. Maybe you are stuck in your career and unmotivated to make a change. These are things that can stress us out! But it's important we remember that God knows the plans for our future, and they are good! Make sure you're talking to Him about your worries. He is the only One who can restore hope.

Always Ready to Listen

When you call me and come and pray to me,
I will listen to you. When you search for me,
yes, search for me with all your heart, you
will find me. I will be present for you, declares
the LORD, and I will end your captivity.

JEREMIAH 29:12-14 CEB

When you're struggling to figure things out and aren't sure whom to talk to, God reminds you He is ready to listen. Scripture plainly says when we call on His name and pray, He hears us. Every time we cry out to God for help, seeking Him above everyone else, we'll find Him. There are few who would make such a promise and none who could follow through like God. Even with the best intentions, it's the Lord alone who will always be present. Let Him be the One to pull you from the bondage of stress. He won't let you down.

The Inevitability of Suffering

*And then, after your brief suffering, the
God of all loving grace, who has called you
to share in his eternal glory in Christ, will
personally and powerfully restore you and
make you stronger than ever. Yes, he will
set you firmly in place and build you up.*

1 PETER 5:10 TPT

No matter how we try to avoid it, suffering is a part of
the human experience. It's inescapable. And it's in these
tough seasons that we learn so much about who we are
and who God is. It allows us to be lacking so we can
clearly see His abundance. It teaches us to depend on
Him over everything and everyone else. And when we
trust that our suffering has an ending and a purpose,
we can endure, knowing He will restore. When you're
feeling stress and worry, cling to this truth. God won't
leave you in it for long.

When You're Afraid and Dismayed

So don't be afraid. I am here, with you;
don't be dismayed, for I am your God. I will
strengthen you, help you. I am here with My
right hand to make right and to hold you up.

ISAIAH 41:10 VOICE

Can we agree that it's sometimes hard to not be afraid and dismayed because life is full of things that evoke these responses? In the blink of an eye, we can go from peaceful to panicked because of a phone call. We can go from faith-filled to fear-filled by a difficult interaction. Our heart can be calm one moment and full of chaos in the next after bad news hits. But the Lord is a constant source of steadiness for us to hold on to. He is with us. He is for us. God promises to strengthen and help by holding us up.

Letting Words Encourage

Anxious fear brings depression, but a life-giving word of encouragement can do wonders to restore joy to the heart.

PROVERBS 12:25 TPT

Just like we need encouragement when we're feeling overwhelmed and stressed out, we should be quick to reassure others in the battle too. It can be a joy-draining situation when we're unsure about what's ahead. It can cause sleepless nights and restless days that keep us destabilized and unable to embrace peace. We may find ourselves full of worry about how it will all work out in the end. Fear and stress take a big toll on our lives, no doubt about it. But when we take to heart the importance of life-giving words for a weary soul, it can be a game changer. Whether for yourself or to inspire someone else, let what you speak give confidence when it's needed the most.

Justice Is God's Alone

But I know that all their evil plans will boomerang back onto them. Every plot they hatch will simply seal their own doom. For you, my God, you will destroy them, giving them what they deserve. For you are my true tower of strength, my safe place, my hideout, and my true shelter.

PSALM 94:22-23 TPT

Don't worry, the ones plotting evil and hate against you will have to answer to God. He will bring justice in His way at the right time. If allowed to prosper, it won't be for long. And in the end, they will get what they deserve. Don't worry about getting even. Don't be nervous or fearful through it. Friend, the concern is not yours to have. Instead, let your faith be what brings peace. Remember you are safe with God. He is your strength and shelter. Rest in Him.

The Choice to Bless at All Times

I will bless the LORD at all times; his praise will always be in my mouth. I praise the LORD—let the suffering listen and rejoice.

PSALM 34:1-2 CEB

Think about it. If you're busy blessing the Lord at all times, you won't have the space to stress. There won't be time to let anxious thoughts run wild. Worry and fear won't have the power to command your time and attention. And when your spirit is unsettled by letdowns, arguments, unmet expectations, and overscheduling, praising the Lord for all He is doing as well as what He promises to do will keep you focused on the right things. Rather than give in to the uneasiness of the situation you're facing, you'll have the confidence to stand strong in faith, knowing the Lord's hand in your life is mighty.

A Benefit of Passionate Pursuit

Worship in awe and wonder, all you who've been made holy! For all who fear him will feast with plenty. Even the strong and the wealthy grow weak and hungry, but those who passionately pursue the Lord will never lack any good thing.

PSALM 34:9-10 TPT

It can be a stressful space when we worry about having enough. It's difficult to stay positive when we don't feel like we have what we need to thrive. But scripture reminds us of a powerful truth. It says the key to never lacking any good thing is choosing to pursue God with passion. It's our respect and worship of who He is that will remove worry. Why? Because we'll know the Lord promises to meet our every need, so we don't have to stress. Never forget God sees you and your lack, and He will take care of both.

More Than Halfway

*GOD met me more than halfway, he freed me
from my anxious fears. Look at him; give him
your warmest smile. Never hide your feelings
from him. When I was desperate, I called
out, and GOD got me out of a tight spot.*

PSALM 34:4-6 MSG

If you ask, God will free you from the fears tangling your
heart. He will release the anxiety that's eating at you.
When you open up and share what's weighing you down,
the Lord will bring you into a new place of freedom. What
a huge relief to know it's not all up to you. When you
take a step toward Him, God will meet you more than
halfway. Worried about your marriage? Anxious about
the upcoming hard conversation? Troubled by the bad
news? Fretting over financial woes? Cry out to God and
let Him be the One to bring peace back to your heart.

When It Feels Impossible

Do you want to live a long, good life, enjoying the beauty that fills each day? Then never speak a lie or allow wicked words to come from your mouth. Keep turning your back on every sin, and make "peace" your life motto. Practice being at peace with everyone.

PSALM 34:12-14 TPT

Does today's verse make your pursuit of a long, good life feel impossible? When it links this possibility to honesty and purity in the words coming from your mouth, do you want to throw in the towel? Does it feel unreasonable to think you can turn your back on every sin, living in peace with everyone? Take a deep breath, and exhale the stress and worry. God isn't asking for your perfection here. He's fully aware that's a hopeless chase. Consider instead that He's asking you to live with purpose, being intentional with your life. With His help, you're set.

God Is Your Bodyguard

God will be your bodyguard to protect you when trouble is near. Not one bone will be broken. Evil will cause the death of the wicked, for they hate and persecute the devoted lovers of God. Make no mistake about it: God will hold them guilty and punish them; they will pay the penalty!

PSALM 34:20-21 TPT

What do you do to protect yourself? What measures are in place to keep you safe from trouble? Do you rely on the government or an agency? Maybe it's a family member or a trusted friend? Maybe it's an alarm system or pepper spray? When we put our faith in worldly things, their ability to reduce our stress is limited. It's short lived. But God will be your bodyguard for the long haul. In His great love and care, He'll be the One to protect you! So be wise, and don't let anxiety drive you to the wrong things.

Why You Can Be Happy

How happy is the one whose wrongs are forgiven, whose sin is hidden from sight. How happy is the person whose sin the Eternal will not take into account. How happy are those who no longer lie, to themselves or others.

PSALM 32:1-2 VOICE

Are you stressing out over the sins you've committed? Are you worried they will be held against you in the end? Friend, if you have received Jesus as your personal Savior and repented of your sins, you have every reason to be happy! Why? Because Jesus' death on the cross paid the price for every sin—past, present, and future—which means you're no longer guilty of them. There is no reason to stress and worry over what God thinks. To Him, the Son's blood has covered them all and washed you clean. So live free and be happy! The debt has been paid!

Close to the Crushed

*The Lord is close to all whose hearts are crushed
by pain, and he is always ready to restore the
repentant one. Even when bad things happen to
the good and godly ones, the Lord will save them
and not let them be defeated by what they face.*

PSALM 34:18-19 TPT

The stress that comes from a broken heart is almost
unbearable. The anxiousness it brings into every part
of our lives is at best overwhelming. And while we may
be frustrated that bad things happen to good people,
it's not theologically sound to think otherwise. There
is reason to celebrate, however, because God promises
to be close to those in pain. He's always ready to save
and restore the faithful. So keep perspective through
the stress and strain from heartaches, because God is
on the move in your life, and you won't be overtaken
by what you're facing.

Their Plan Won't Prevail

Then my enemies shall turn back and scatter on the day I call out to You. This I know for certain: God is on my side. In God whose word I praise and in the Eternal whose word I praise—In God I have placed my trust. I shall not let fear come in, for what can measly men do to me?

PSALM 56:9-11 VOICE

Friend, don't let them stress you out. While weapons may be formed against you, they will not prosper. While others may plan and plot, God sees every detail. With the Lord on your side, how can anyone pull one over on you? So go ahead and place your trust in Him. Be courageous, unwilling to entertain fear. No one can ever trump God's plan for you. Even more, there's no real reason to worry because your faith anchors you to the One who is eternal, and His love never fails.

Stressed That He Will Walk Away

*For the Lord will never walk away from
his cherished ones, nor would he forsake
his chosen ones who belong to him.*

PSALM 94:14 TPT

Do you ever stress out, worrying that God will walk away? Are you concerned, thinking you've outsinned others and God's about to dump you in frustration? Maybe your offense was a betrayal toward your husband. Maybe you yelled again at your child after promising to stop. Maybe you ignored the budget and now you're broke. Or maybe you didn't show up when your friend needed you the most. Deep down, you feel like you've disappointed God, and it's an unsettling feeling. While our earthly community may choose to walk away, the Lord never will. Scripture is clear when it says God won't ever forsake His chosen ones—and that's you. No matter what we've done, our relationship to the Father is secure and safe.

It's a Game Changer

Tormented and empty are wicked and destructive people, but the one who trusts in the Eternal is wrapped tightly in His gracious love. Express your joy; be happy in Him, you who are good and true. Go ahead, shout and rejoice aloud, you whose hearts are honest and straightforward.

PSALM 32:10-11 VOICE

When the weight of worry begins to bear down on you, it's the perfect time to express your joy. Rather than give in to the stress of situations, choose to be happy in Him! This isn't always easy to do, but it can be a game changer. There's no room for anxiety when you're trying to walk out your faith. So be aware when it tries to infiltrate your thoughts, making you doubt God's sovereignty and goodness. Be honest with yourself, and ask Him to search your heart for anything that might keep you from peace.

He Keeps Track

*You've kept track of my every toss and turn
through the sleepless nights, each tear entered
in your ledger, each ache written in your book.*

PSALM 56:8 MSG

It's powerful to think the Lord is fully aware of every tear that you've cried. Be it from a broken heart or a stressful situation, God notices when you cry and keeps track in His holy ledger. Because He loves and cares for you so deeply, He keeps an eye on His beloved. He sees when you're anxious. He knows when you're nervous. When you're frightened, God takes note. When you're concerned or hesitant, He understands why. Nothing escapes Him, especially when it comes to you. So turn to the Lord in those hard moments. Let Him bring perspective and a sense of peace. Let God calm your anxious heart.

Asking for His Comfort

*When anxiety overtakes me and worries
are many, Your comfort lightens my soul.*

PSALM 94:19 VOICE

When we let our minds wander down the road and into tomorrow, our stress often multiplies. We begin to make up stories based on our feelings and what we think may be happening. We assume we will fail, that someone will leave, or the outcome is going to be nothing short of terrible. Rather than live in freedom, we are full of anxiety that keeps us stirred up day and night. Instead of standing in strength, we crumble in fear and worry. And God is right there waiting for us to ask for help. He is listening for your cry. The Lord is ready and willing to intervene on your behalf. So don't waste any time in asking for His comfort, because it will lighten your soul every time.

Always Room for You

Don't get lost in despair; believe in God, and keep on believing in Me. My Father's home is designed to accommodate all of you. If there were not room for everyone, I would have told you that. I am going to make arrangements for your arrival. I will be there to greet you personally and welcome you home, where we will be together.

JOHN 14:1–3 VOICE

Sometimes we feel like we don't belong—like there is no room for us. We decide we don't fit in and feel the stress from being outcasts. We may have been rejected in a relationship, abandoned by a parent, excluded by a group, or turned down for a job. But God reminds us that if we're saved, there's a place for us in heaven, and Jesus will be waiting with a welcome. We may feel the stress from earthly rebuffs, but our eternal homecoming will be full of love and acceptance.

Let God Be on Your Team

Take my side, God—I'm getting kicked around, stomped on every day. Not a day goes by but somebody beats me up; they make it their duty to beat me up. When I get really afraid I come to you in trust. I'm proud to praise God; fearless now, I trust in God. What can mere mortals do?

PSALM 56:1-4 MSG

Do you remember as a kid (maybe even as an adult) trying to get others on your side during arguments? In your deep insecurity, you recruited friends and family to help you stand your ground. You needed a posse of people to make you feel stronger. And you thought having a team would quiet the stress and worry battling inside. But it never really did. Let God be the One you want instead. He can calm your anxious thoughts, bring peace and perspective, and help heal what's broken.

The Power of His Presence

"Be strong and courageous, do not be
afraid or tremble in dread before them,
for it is the LORD your God who goes with
you. He will not fail you or abandon you."

DEUTERONOMY 31:6 AMP

No matter what's stressing you out, don't be afraid. Regardless of the anxious thoughts trying to invade, refuse to feel dread. This may feel impossible, but it's completely attainable when you trust the Lord. It's easy to underestimate the power His presence provides, because we get overwhelmed by the circumstances at hand. But be careful. When God tells us to be strong and courageous, He knows the only way we can walk it out is with Him. Our humanness is flawed and limited. Cling to the truth that He is always with you, will never fail or abandon you, and will help you be brave, and you will have the confidence you need for the next step.

Giving Burdens to God

*"Are you weary, carrying a heavy burden?
Come to me. I will refresh your life, for I am
your oasis. Simply join your life with mine.
Learn my ways and you'll discover that I'm
gentle, humble, easy to please. You will find
refreshment and rest in me. For all that I require
of you will be pleasant and easy to bear."*

MATTHEW 11:28-30 TPT

What heavy burden are you carrying today? Did test results reveal a concern? Are you struggling to make ends meet financially? Did you lose a husband and are grieving the loss? Are you troubled by the state of the nation? Did your hopes fall through? Are your friendships a source of stress? Right now, take every burden to God. He's inviting you into His peace. He promises to bring comfort. Yes, it takes courage to release these things, but it's the only way you will find true rest and refreshment.

God Calls You by Name

But now, says the LORD—the one who created
you, Jacob, the one who formed you, Israel:
Don't fear, for I have redeemed you; I have
called you by name; you are mine.

ISAIAH 43:1 CEB

To think God has called you by name is overwhelming at times. Of all the people in the world—past, present, and future—the Creator knows *your* name. Even more, He calls you His. Don't allow the stress of being celebrated and seen weigh you down. As women, one of the biggest desires of our hearts is for someone to care enough to know us. It tangles every insecurity and rustles up every fear to think we may be a nobody. But friend, you are known by the greatest of all times. The King of kings knows your blueprint because He created you with divine complexity, and you are branded as His beloved.

A Tweak in Mindset

So no matter what your task is, work hard. Always do your best as the Lord's servant, not as man's, because you know your reward is the Lord's inheritance. You serve the Lord, the Anointed One, and anyone who does wrong will be paid his due because He doesn't play favorites.

COLOSSIANS 3:23-25 VOICE

Rather than getting stirred up by endless requests for help or engaging in situations that feel impossible, choose to adopt a new mindset. Consider you are working for God instead of humankind. That minor tweak in thought changes how we see the situation and helps remove the stress because we drop any offense. Instead, we adopt a servant's heart. We may be helping others, but we are serving God through the work we're doing. And when our hearts are in the right place, it's God who will be glorified.

His Presence Is Permanent

When you pass through the waters, I will be with you; when through the rivers, they won't sweep over you. When you walk through the fire, you won't be scorched and flame won't burn you. I am the LORD your God, the holy one of Israel, your savior.

ISAIAH 43:2-3 CEB

Don't worry, friend; you're not alone, although it may feel that way right now. The fear may be more than you can handle, and no one seems to care. Some may have walked away in frustration, leaving you without help. You may be battling feelings of abandonment as the ones you trusted to be there aren't. As if the stress of the situation weren't enough, you feel isolated. But the truth is you are held! God promises to be with you always no matter what. When no one else is around, remember His presence is permanent!

Worry Prayers versus Confident Prayers

*If you don't know what you're doing, pray
to the Father. He loves to help. You'll get his
help, and won't be condescended to when
you ask for it. Ask boldly, believingly, without
a second thought. People who "worry their
prayers" are like wind-whipped waves.*

JAMES 1:5–7 MSG

Make no mistake, God wants to hear exactly what's
on your heart—anytime, anywhere. But part of having
faith means your prayers mature so you're not always
praying panicked. There will be unhinged moments,
yes. There will be good reasons for it at times! But at
some point, we need to rise above the wind-whipped
waves and let our faith kick in. We need to trust the
Lord knows the details and is in control. And our *worry
prayers* need to morph into *confident prayers* because
we know without a doubt He's with us and will help us.

When Your Quest Is to Win

Be even-tempered, content with second place, quick to forgive an offense. Forgive as quickly and completely as the Master forgave you. And regardless of what else you put on, wear love. It's your basic, all-purpose garment. Never be without it.

COLOSSIANS 3:13–14 MSG

Are you competitive, always pushing for the win? Is being better than everyone else your goal? It may work on the tennis court but not in your marriage. It might be a fantastic motivator in school or in the job market, but it fails as a goal in parenting. Why? Because that kind of pursuit doesn't promote the idea of loving others. It makes forgiveness almost impossible because we lack a heart of reconciliation. And the stress that comes from always wanting to be on top will do us in. Ask God for contentment so your quest isn't about winning but loving.

The Gift of Adversity

*Consider it a sheer gift, friends, when tests
and challenges come at you from all sides.
You know that under pressure, your faith-life is
forced into the open and shows its true colors.
So don't try to get out of anything prematurely.
Let it do its work so you become mature and
well-developed, not deficient in any way.*

JAMES 1:2–4 MSG

Today's verse is asking us to change our perspective. Rather than stress out when tests and challenges are bombarding us, we should instead embrace them. It's the pressure from these seasons that deepens our trust in God. It matures our faith in the only One who can bring beauty from ashes. And when we stay present in the pressure, releasing the tendency to control and manipulate, our stress is replaced with His peace. The adversity may still be difficult and messy to navigate, but we don't have to be overwhelmed by it.

The Stress of Lies

Don't lie to one another. You're done with that old life. It's like a filthy set of ill-fitting clothes you've stripped off and put in the fire. Now you're dressed in a new wardrobe. Every item of your new way of life is custom-made by the Creator, with his label on it. All the old fashions are now obsolete.

COLOSSIANS 3:9-10 MSG

Few things are more stressful than keeping track of lies told. Regardless of why we weren't truthful, it's hard to perpetuate a lie because it's easy to forget where we left off. Every time we're around the person to whom we lied, we're racked with anxiety, making each interaction uncomfortable. Scripture says when we become a Christian, we're done with that kind of living. It's like wearing clothes that no longer fit. Friend, embrace the new wardrobe that comes with faith and choose to be a truth teller. Remove the stress lying brings.

Listen First, Speak Second

My dearest brothers and sisters, take this to heart: Be quick to listen, but slow to speak. And be slow to become angry, for human anger is never a legitimate tool to promote God's righteous purpose.

JAMES 1:19-20 TPT

Sometimes in our stress and fear, we are anything but slow to speak. We aren't quick to listen because we're busy giving someone an earful of our frustration. Rather than gather all the information to fully understand the situation, we jump to conclusions and act right then and there. We make assumptions without concern for the truth. And if we were to be completely honest, we sometimes heap irritation and anxiety from other issues into the current matter, blowing it all out of proportion. God's desire is for you to listen first and speak second. He knows your anger won't point others toward Him, but the Lord is hoping your intentional faith will.

The Tension

And that means killing off everything connected with that way of death: sexual promiscuity, impurity, lust, doing whatever you feel like whenever you feel like it, and grabbing whatever attracts your fancy. That's a life shaped by things and feelings instead of by God.

COLOSSIANS 3:5-6 MSG

As a Christian, there will always be a felt tension between the call of our fleshy desires and the call to walk in the ways of God. One of the biggest lies the Enemy tells us is that following God is boring and dull, so in rebellion to the humdrum, we sometimes shape our life by things. After that moment of excitement, we feel the tug of guilt and anxiety. There's so much goodness in store when we release the world's attraction and go all-in with God, including relief from stress and fear. Ask for His help to embrace the adventure of a godly life.

Well-Formed Love

There is no room in love for fear. Well-formed love banishes fear. Since fear is crippling, a fearful life—fear of death, fear of judgment— is one not yet fully formed in love.
1 JOHN 4:18 MSG

When we fully embrace God's love for us, we'll be able to trust in the truth that He'll always care for our needs. The two go hand in hand. It's hard to have faith when we don't feel love. We can't trust when we feel insecure with someone's true feelings toward us. And the anxiety that comes from this instability can be overwhelming at best. Sometimes it's hard to believe God can love us, because we're so imperfect. To be honest, we've never experienced well-formed love here on earth. But as you mature in faith, the realization of God's care and compassion will help you release stress and embrace the love He has for you.

Act Like It

*So if you're serious about living this new
resurrection life with Christ, act like it.
Pursue the things over which Christ presides.
Don't shuffle along, eyes to the ground,
absorbed with the things right in front of
you. Look up, and be alert to what is going
on around Christ—that's where the action
is. See things from his perspective.*

COLOSSIANS 3:1-2 MSG

Whoa. Paul's call to let our actions reflect our faith is powerful. It's not a mere suggestion or hint. He's issuing a challenge for believers to live out their faith. Our lives should show we're serious about our belief. And if we choose to pursue a righteous life, then walking around stressed out won't work. We can't live defeated with heads hung low. Instead, we should exude confidence and excitement, knowing God is working in the difficult situations we're facing. And our eyes should be focused on Him alone.

Does It Line Up?

Delightfully loved friends, don't trust every spirit, but carefully examine what they say to determine if they are of God, because many false prophets have mingled into the world. Here's the test for those with the genuine Spirit of God: they will confess Jesus as the Christ who has come in the flesh.

1 JOHN 4:1–2 TPT

Rather than worry if what you're hearing from someone is true, ask God for clarity. Look in His Word to see if what you're hearing aligns with scripture. If they don't believe Jesus is the Son of God who came to earth to pay the price for your sins and bridge the gap sin caused in your relationship with God, run in the other direction. Remember that when you follow His words, peace will reign in your heart. When you don't, the result will be stress and fear.

The Connection between Peace and Jesus

Let the peace of Christ [the inner calm of one who walks daily with Him] be the controlling factor in your hearts [deciding and settling questions that arise]. To this peace indeed you were called as members in one body [of believers]. And be thankful [to God always].

COLOSSIANS 3:15 AMP

The truth is that peace and stress can't coexist. When we choose to let the peace of Jesus be our operating system, stress has no option but to stay at bay. Being ruled by a sense of His comfort keeps anxiety from creeping into our thoughts and stirring us up. Rather than let the weight of worry press down on us, we stay calm by making time with God a priority every day. So be aware of the connection between peace and Jesus. And make sure you're following the path to them both.

God Is Coming

Strengthen the weak hands, and support the unsteady knees. Say to those who are panicking: "Be strong! Don't fear! Here's your God, coming with vengeance; with divine retribution God will come to save you."

ISAIAH 35:3-4 CEB

Don't worry. God is coming to save you. At the moment, it may not feel like it; but at the right time and in the right way, the Lord will exact His divine retribution. When you're worried they will get away with what they've done, rest knowing they'll have to answer to God. When you feel stressed no one will show up for you, be strong and wait for Him. He won't leave you in this mess. So ask the Lord to give you strength and steady your stance in faith. Let Him be the reason you can camp in calm rather than drown in distress.

Truths to Melt the Stress

*Your beauty and love chase after me
every day of my life. I'm back home in
the house of GOD for the rest of my life.*

PSALM 23:6 MSG

Maybe you worry your life will always be a mess, just like it is now. Maybe you're concerned you'll always be sad or depressed. Are you thinking you will fail at the things you try to do? When you instead choose to stand firm in your faith, you will learn what it means to walk through life with the Lord. You'll be able to see God's goodness and the ways you've been blessed by it. And you'll be enriched by the effects of His love—a constant force and factor in how you see yourself. Even more, you'll recognize eternal life will be with God in heaven. Together, these truths will melt the stress of the day and calm your anxious heart.

Every Need Met

*And my God will liberally supply (fill
until full) your every need according to
His riches in glory in Christ Jesus.*
PHILIPPIANS 4:19 AMP

Every time a worry pops into your mind about a potential unmet need, give it to God. When you're concerned about the amount of bills piling up, tell Him about it. When you're scared marriage or kids won't ever happen for you, take it to the Lord first. Every time you feel anxious about finding friends, He needs to hear it from your mouth. God will meet those needs according to His will. And that means His plan may be different than yours. But every *no* is only because there is a better *yes* down the road. So keep praying and asking and thanking God in advance. He knows every need and already has a plan in place to meet it.

You'll Be in a Better Position

You serve me a six-course dinner right in front of my enemies. You revive my drooping head; my cup brims with blessing.

PSALM 23:5 MSG

Just when you think evil will always win, you come across a verse like this. These words are why we don't drown in depression or sulk in stress. This is why we can hold our heads high and keep positive no matter what's happening around us. As scripture powerfully reveals, there will come a time where God evens the playing field. His favor will be on full display. You will find yourself in a much better position than those who have tried to bring you down. And your faithfulness will be met with abundance. In His love and care for you, the Lord will revive your weary heart and bless you. Evil will not win in the end, so choose peace over stress.

Working All Things Together

We are assured and know that [God being a partner in their labor] all things work together and are [fitting into a plan] for good to and for those who love God and are called according to [His] design and purpose.

ROMANS 8:28 AMPC

God has a beautiful and powerful way of bringing all things together for good. Let this be encouragement to not live with overwhelming anxiety. In this life, you will have trouble. Relationships will be messy. Finances will falter. Your health will fail. Hopes and dreams won't always come to pass in the ways we want. But God assures us that He has a plan for our benefit. Not only that, this plan is good. Do you love the Lord? Then you can count on this promise. When things are stressful and frustrating and you're maxed out, let your faith remind you God is with you, working everything to your benefit.

When We Go through the Valleys

Even when the way goes through Death Valley,
I'm not afraid when you walk at my side. Your
trusty shepherd's crook makes me feel secure.
PSALM 23:4 MSG

Deep breath, friend. God is with you right now. Whether on the mountaintop or in the dark valley, He is with you. Let that truth comfort you when everything feels overwhelming. Grab His arm, stay close, and let Him lead you through the mess. Not only does God know the details of the journey, He also knows the best way to walk it out. We don't have to be filled with anxiety; our Shepherd will guide and protect us along the way. And when we begin to feel scared, we can grab on even tighter as we follow His lead. The valleys are part of life, but they don't have to unravel us.

Just Wait!

That's why I don't think there's any comparison between the present hard times and the coming good times. The created world itself can hardly wait for what's coming next.

ROMANS 8:18-19 MSG

You may be feeling the crushing weight of worry right now. Are you stressed about the state of your marriage and what to do next? Is your concern over a child who's having a rough school year yet again? Maybe you're scared about the direction of the nation or even your own community. It may be apprehension over an unwanted change you can't control. There's no doubt we will face difficult situations and seasons when we want to give up or give in. But don't forget scripture tells us any depth of destruction we may face will be incomparable to the bounty of beautiful times coming our way. His goodness is ahead, so stay strong and faithful!

When All Your Needs Are Met

GOD, my shepherd! I don't need a thing.
You have bedded me down in lush meadows,
you find me quiet pools to drink from. True
to your word, you let me catch my breath
and send me in the right direction.
PSALM 23:1-3 MSG

Imagine being in a place where you don't need a thing. You feel loved and cared for. Your immediate physical and tangible needs are covered. Where there used to be stress and fear about life, you are comforted by God's presence. Friend, this can be your reality even when everything around you feels tornadic. In the middle of chaos, it's possible to catch your breath and find direction. And when you recognize your need for God's leadership and provision, He'll honor your faith. You'll be able to experience the kind of lasting fulfillment and emotional stability that come from surrendering to the Lord.

His Perfect and Absolute Peace

*Perfect, absolute peace surrounds those
whose imaginations are consumed with
you; they confidently trust in you.*
ISAIAH 26:3 TPT

When you need to stop the stinkin' thinkin' because
it's robbing you of peace, intentionally think about the
Lord. Reflect on the times He saved you from a painful
situation. Contemplate how He provided money for
groceries when you had none or how He led you out
of messy circumstances. Remember moments where
joy miraculously replaced doom and gloom or when
you knew He was speaking to you through consistent,
persistent messages. Can you recall having a boost
of bravery when you needed it the most? Or finding
confidence to speak up for yourself or someone else?
Be deliberate to change the direction of thought to the
goodness of God, and feel the perfect and absolute
peace surround your heart once again.

The Spirit Pleads Our Case

In the same way, the Spirit comes to help our weakness. We don't know what we should pray, but the Spirit himself pleads our case with unexpressed groans. The one who searches hearts knows how the Spirit thinks, because he pleads for the saints, consistent with God's will.

ROMANS 8:26-27 CEB

Sometimes our stress comes from not knowing what to pray. We can't always describe what we're feeling. We may not have all the details surrounding our mess, so we don't see the full picture of what's happening. Our prayers may be nothing but liquid words as the tears spill out. And we may not even understand why we're worked up. But God knew this! And that's why the Spirit is there to plead our case to Him. So take a deep breath and exhale the anxiety, because God has all the information and a plan to help.

Our Fortress of Protection

*The Eternal is my light amidst my darkness
and my rescue in times of trouble. So whom
shall I fear? He surrounds me with a fortress of
protection. So nothing should cause me alarm.*

PSALM 27:1 VOICE

It's funny to think of how easily we're alarmed these days. Some of us are calm and steady, but most of us freak out pretty easily and regularly. Think back over this week, friend. What has alarmed you and caused worry? How did you respond? Where was God in the mix? What a relief to know it's the Lord who will help us stand strong, so we don't have to try so hard ourselves. He is the light we can follow when things get dark. God promises to surround us with His protection, so rather than be jolted by fear, we can be full of divine confidence.

It Won't Succeed

What then shall we say to all these things? If God is for us, who can be [successful] against us? He who did not spare [even] His own Son, but gave Him up for us all, how will He not also, along with Him, graciously give us all things?

ROMANS 8:31-32 AMP

In your lifetime, there will be many things to bring fear, worry, and anxiety. People will plot, and situations will get out of hand. You'll get an unexpected punch in the gut by heartache—chances are you already have. There will be unflattering gossip spread by those you thought were friends, all to bring into question your reputation. Relationships will sour and end. But take heart! Since God is for you, these trials and tribulations won't be successful! You will feel the sting, but God will save and restore you every time.

Focused on the End Prize

*I am pleading with the Eternal for this one thing,
my soul's desire: to live with Him all of my days—in
the shadow of His temple, to behold His beauty and
ponder His ways in the company of His people.*

PSALM 27:4 VOICE

How would your stress level diminish today if you kept
your thoughts focused on the end prize of life in heaven
with the Lord? Would it give you perspective of the value
in staying engaged with God right now? Would it give
you courage to activate your faith and follow His lead?
Would your heart be filled with hope of things to come?
Regardless of the ugly things we will have to inevitably
deal with during our time on earth, we can be excited
and expectant for the awesomeness of eternity. Let it
be what drives your worries away once and for all.

More Than a Conqueror

Yet even in the midst of all these things, we triumph over them all, for God has made us to be more than conquerors, and his demonstrated love is our glorious victory over everything!

ROMANS 8:37 TPT

When you put your trust in God and let Him lead you through the messy middle, you will find victory on the other side. No matter what you're struggling with, having the Lord on your team always gives you a leg up. It assures you won't stay trapped in the pit of despair. It guarantees stress won't overtake you. Worry won't be able to weigh you down. And because God has made us to be more than conquerors, when we mix that with His unmatched love, we'll experience a glorious victory over whatever comes our way. We will find the peace we've been missing, and our hearts won't be overwhelmed with hopelessness.

At the End of Ourselves

I cannot shout any louder. Eternal One—hear my cry and respond with Your grace. The prodding of my heart leads me to chase after You. I am seeking You, Eternal One—don't retreat from me.
PSALM 27:7-8 VOICE

Can you hear the desperation in the psalmist's words? It's such a tough place to be, but we understand the level of anxiety that comes from getting to the end of ourselves. In desperation, we've exhausted every bit of energy to right what's wrong. We've looked at every angle, hoping to find a path to relief. We've tried with all our might to fix the circumstances dragging us down, but we're still here in the mess. Just like the psalmist, this is when we know God is our only hope. Let the Lord be the source of help you cling to always. Trust Him to be your hope!

You Are Solid with God

*So now I live with the confidence that there
is nothing in the universe with the power to
separate us from God's love. I'm convinced that
his love will triumph over death, life's troubles,
fallen angels, or dark rulers in the heavens.
There is nothing in our present or future
circumstances that can weaken his love.*

ROMANS 8:38 TPT

When you're worried God is done with you, reread today's verse. Let it be what keeps you strong in your faith of His love for you. Notice what Paul says about it. He states there's nothing that can pull God's love from us. He says it'll have victory over death, any of life's troubles, and all angels and rulers of darkness. And even more, nothing will ever be able to remove the potency of it. So take heart and hold on, trusting you are solid with the Lord and nothing can change it!

Fear of Rejection and Abandonment

You've always been right there for me; don't turn your back on me now. Don't throw me out, don't abandon me; you've always kept the door open. My father and mother walked out and left me, but GOD took me in.

PSALM 27:9-10 MSG

This important passage of scripture speaks directly to fears associated with rejection and abandonment. Few things cause more stress and strife in our life than feeling forsaken; at the core of who we are, we crave connection and community. And when it seems we're being discarded, it delivers a sting like nothing else. Friend, know that when you lose earthly relationships for whatever reason, God's love for you remains steady. When things are shaky on earth, His compassion for you never is. And release anxiety that says you're not worthy of love, because God sent Jesus to earth to secure it.

His Love Is a Force

*There is no power above us or beneath us—
no power that could ever be found in the
universe that can distance us from God's
passionate love, which is lavished upon us
through our Lord Jesus, the Anointed One!*

ROMANS 8:39 TPT

God's love is a commanding force to be reckoned with because there is nothing aside from Him that can command it. No one else has the power to change, cancel, or redirect it. God's love cannot be manipulated or controlled. It's steady, unable to be increased or decreased. His love is completely unconditional and undemanding. And while we may run from it at times because we feel unworthy, we'll never be able to get distance from it. Rest, friend, and calm your fears. God's love for you is unshakable and unmovable. Even more, He lavished it on you through His Son, Jesus Christ, thanks to His work on the cross.

Stay with God

I'm sure now I'll see God's goodness in the exuberant earth. Stay with GOD! Take heart. Don't quit. I'll say it again: Stay with GOD.
PSALM 27:13–14 MSG

Stay with God. In the psalmist's mind, this powerful statement was worthy of repeating because he needed it to stick. So often we veer away from God and look for immediate results from worldly offerings. When we are anxious, we want our hearts calmed right away. When afraid, we want instantaneous peace. When battling worry, our hope is for a quick remedy to make it all go away. But the minute we turn in the opposite direction from God, things fall apart. The world's solutions offer nothing good that lasts. We may feel temporary relief, but soon the anxiety comes flooding back with a vengeance. Stay with God and see His goodness!

The Web of Worry

Then Jesus said to his disciples, "Therefore, I say to you, don't worry about your life, what you will eat, or about your body, what you will wear. There is more to life than food and more to the body than clothing. Consider the ravens: they neither plant nor harvest, they have no silo or barn, yet God feeds them. You are worth so much more than birds!"

LUKE 12:22-24 CEB

When Jesus says not to worry, it's a tall order. For many, worry is a companion. We worry when our teenager takes the car out or about upcoming college expenses. We worry about the performance review we're about to have. We worry about how we'll battle loneliness now that we're single again. And when we take our eyes off the Lord, forgetting He's our source for peace and strength, we find ourselves tangled in the web of worry every time.

Always Be Ready to Explain

But give reverent honor in your hearts to the Anointed One and treat him as the holy Master of your lives. And if anyone asks about the hope living within you, always be ready to explain your faith.

1 PETER 3:15 TPT

Let your hope in God be what encourages others to make better choices for themselves. When you choose to trust Him with the stress and strife in your own life, don't forget it has the power to inspire those around you to press into God too. When they see your faith reign over fear, they'll want to know your secret sauce so they can be confident as well. It's important to realize the value of living out loud for all to see, because your example can lead others to freedom. Always be ready to explain your faith that leads you down the path of peace.

Worrying Helps Nothing

"Who among you by worrying can add a single moment to your life? If you can't do such a small thing, why worry about the rest?"
LUKE 12:25–26 CEB

Point taken—worrying helps nothing! Giving in to stress doesn't fix a thing. And partnering with anxiety can't improve our situation or life. So why are we investing so much time in something that will provide no fruit? Why do we continue to place our hope in the wrong thing? Let's decide to break the habit and instead give every worry and fear to God because He knows exactly what needs to happen. He understands the root causes and the end solutions, so we don't have to figure it all out. If you want a less stressed life, the Lord is your only hope. Surrender your anxious heart, and choose to trust that God will bring peace to the chaos inside.

Don't Be Intimidated

Why would anyone harm you if you're passionate and devoted to pleasing God? But even if you happen to suffer for doing what is right, you will have the joyful experience of the blessing of God. And don't be intimidated or terrified by those who would terrify you.

1 PETER 3:13-14 TPT

Peer pressure to follow the crowd is no laughing matter. Group think and a mob mentality are real. When you choose to stay on the narrow path of faith, the stress from ridicule can be overwhelming at times. It's that suffering that often causes us to be intimidated, giving in rather than standing our ground. Friend, there will always be naysayers against your faith, but the stress doesn't have permission to sway you unless you allow it. Let God be your strength in those times. Let Him build your confidence and courage so anxious thoughts can't control you.

Farming Faithfulness

Don't get upset over evildoers; don't be jealous of those who do wrong, because they will fade fast, like grass; they will wither like green vegetables. Trust the LORD and do good; live in the land, and farm faithfulness. Enjoy the LORD, and he will give what your heart asks.

PSALM 37:1-4 CEB

Sometimes we think the grass is greener in the other pasture. We find ourselves jealous of the crops others are producing. Maybe they do whatever they want without guilt or shame. Maybe they push every limit and toe every line. The big lie is that the path of faith is boring and confining and stressful to walk out. But when we trust God to help us live and love well, He'll bless our heart's desire according to His will. When we choose to farm faithfulness rather than live for ourselves, we will reap the crop of His goodness!

When It's above Our Pay Grade

The Eternal saves His faithful; He lends His strength in hard times; the Eternal comes and frees them—frees them from evildoers and saves them for eternity—simply because they seek shelter in Him.
PSALM 37:39-40 VOICE

We all need help from time to time. Life is full of situations we feel are way above our pay grade. We have only so much strength. We can tolerate only so much before we burst. And eventually, the stress and fear will eat us alive. We just can't navigate the hard times on our own—at least not for long. What a relief to know we aren't expected to! When we need Him, God will show up and free those who love and place their faith in Him. Every time we cry out for the Lord's help, seeking shelter in Him alone, we can trust it will come to be.

The Power of Validation

Open up before GOD, keep nothing back;
he'll do whatever needs to be done: he'll
validate your life in the clear light of day
and stamp you with approval at high noon.

PSALM 37:5-6 MSG

You know what combats stress like a boss? Validation! When someone confirms what we're feeling is real and true, it allows us to exhale. When our words are authenticated, we're no longer crushed under the weight of worrying whether we're believed or not. And every time our fears are substantiated, it helps to calm our anxious heart. But the most important validation comes from God. Be open and honest with the Lord about stress and strife. Let Him be the One to justify and defend you. Since you already have it, let God's approval be the only one you want or care about. Adopting this way of living will allow you to thrive in peace and comfort.

He'll Do It Again

*I commanded Joshua at that time, "You've seen
with your own two eyes everything GOD, your God,
has done to these two kings. GOD is going to do the
same thing to all the kingdoms over there across
the river where you're headed. Don't be afraid of
them. GOD, your God—he's fighting for you."*

DEUTERONOMY 3:21-22 MSG

If God has done it once, there's a precedent in place,
so boldly ask Him to do it again. Let that be what you
pray to the Father when you're worried. When you're
scared things won't turn out okay, remind the Lord what
He's done before and ask Him to repeat it. Maybe you
need the Red Sea in your life to part. Maybe you need
Him to shut the mouths of the lions in your life like He
did for Daniel. Ask God to duplicate His divine acts by
giving examples.

Quiet and Prayerful before God

*Quiet down before GOD, be prayerful before him.
Don't bother with those who climb the ladder,
who elbow their way to the top. Bridle your anger,
trash your wrath, cool your pipes—it only makes
things worse. Before long the crooks will be
bankrupt; GOD-investors will soon own the store.*
PSALM 37:7–9 MSG

Every time your attention is drawn toward the ladder-climbers around you, find the space to be still before God. As your anger and frustration build while watching others claw and elbow their way to the top, intentionally retreat into prayer. These are well-placed traps of stress you should avoid at all costs. Remember, being judge and jury is not your job. Being critical of others does nothing to help your heart or the situation at hand. Instead, be quick to drop those bothers at His feet and go about your business.

Pouring His Peace

Now, may the Lord himself, the Lord of peace, pour into you his peace in every circumstance and in every possible way. The Lord's tangible presence be with you all.

2 THESSALONIANS 3:16 TPT

Oh, let it be, friend! What a beautiful and powerful picture of how much God cares about you. Imagine the amount of heartache you could avoid by asking the Lord to pour His peace into your heart. Think of how it would calm those frayed nerves and bring rest to sleepless nights. Regardless of the stress-filled circumstance, you would be able to experience a deep sense of serenity. Your fears would be quieted by His presence. All apprehension would be met by tranquility. Right now, close your eyes and tell God what has you stirred up. Then ask Him to fill you with the peace of Jesus so you can catch your breath from its effects.

You Will Not Fall

If you are right with God, He strengthens you for the journey; the Eternal will be pleased with your life. And even though you trip up, you will not fall on your face because He holds you by the hand.

PSALM 37:23–24 VOICE

How wonderful to know God will hold your hand through the journey. Just like any good father, He'll keep you close when your relationship with Him is solid. And while you may trip up on the wrong things from time to time, God will steady your step so you won't fall on your face in guilt or shame. You don't have to sit in the stress of trying to figure everything out on your own. This journey of life is meant to be taken with the Lord's help. His strength and wisdom are key. And your pursuit of faith over fear will delight His heart.

From Where Does Your Strength Come?

I look up to the mountains; does my strength come from mountains? No, my strength comes from GOD, who made heaven, and earth, and mountains. He won't let you stumble, your Guardian God won't fall asleep.

PSALM 121:1–3 MSG

Your strength comes from God alone. You may think it results from good, encouraging friendships. You may decide it's your awesome marriage that strengthens you or even that your church group is responsible for it. You may even think it's because you're brave and able to muster the grit yourself. These are all wonderful to have, but they're flawed because they can fail. They aren't guaranteed. And it's stressful when they fall flat, especially when we've put our faith in them. But friend, peace will settle in your spirit when you depend on God above all else. Let Him be your source.

Choose God's Way over Yours

If you truly want to dwell forever in God's presence, forsake evil and do what is right in his eyes. The Lord loves it when he sees us walking in his justice. He will never desert his devoted lovers; they will be kept forever in his faithful care, but the descendants of the wicked will be banished.

PSALM 37:27-28 TPT

Keep today's scripture close by as a constant reminder to choose God's way above your own. Whenever you think you're smarter or wiser, take a moment to reread it. When you feel sneaky enough to try to pull one over on God, remember that nothing escapes His gaze. It's the anxiousness that comes from deliberately ignoring God's way—especially when we know better—that will drive us nuts. Friend, it's just not worth it. Instead, choose the path of the faithful, know He loves to see it, and live without the stress disobedience brings.

God Will Guard You

*GOD's your Guardian, right at your side to protect
you—shielding you from sunstroke, sheltering
you from moonstroke. GOD guards you from
every evil, he guards your very life. He guards
you when you leave and when you return,
he guards you now, he guards you always.*

PSALM 121:5-8 MSG

Notice how many times the word *guard* appears in today's scripture passage. God often speaks in persistent and consistent messages, so pay close attention to what nugget we can glean from the psalmist. As women, we want to feel a sense of security. We aren't wimps; we just appreciate personal safety, and it's stressful when we feel unsafe. Let this verse bring comfort to your anxious heart and remind you God guards you from evil. He guards your life. He guards as you come and go. He will always guard you. And friend, He is guarding you right now.

The Value of Wise Counsel

God-lovers make the best counselors. Their words
possess wisdom and are right and trustworthy.
The ways of God are in their hearts and they won't
swerve from the paths of steadfast righteousness.
PSALM 37:30-31 TPT

Be careful whom you allow to speak into your life. There are many people who may care about you and want what's best. You may have countless references of well-loved therapists. But choose wisely! It's important to receive wise counsel from someone who has the same foundation in the Lord that you do. If they aren't pointing you to the only One who can truly save, they aren't doing you any favors. Looking to anyone or anything but God means you are missing out on divine help and healing. You will be dealing with not only situational stress but also with the heartache that comes from corrupted counsel. Be wise as you choose your support team.

An Assurance and Confidence

Faith is the assurance of things you have hoped for, the absolute conviction that there are realities you've never seen. It was by faith that our forebears were approved. Through faith we understand that the universe was created by the word of God; everything we now see was fashioned from that which is invisible.

HEBREWS 11:1-3 VOICE

Faith is a choice. You choose to be sure of the things you have hoped for. It's an assurance, a confidence that God will deliver. And you decide to believe something is real, even if you can't see it. And there is a powerful conviction with someone who is faith filled. We can read countless stories in the Word about our ancestors who were. Even more, the choice to trust God is why stress doesn't win. It's why worry stays at bay. So cling to it, choosing to believe He'll come through no matter what.

Choosing to Wait Well

*Wait for the Eternal. Keep to His path. Mind
His will. He will come for you, exalt you;
you will inherit the land. Before your very
eyes you will see the end of the wicked.*
PSALM 37:34 VOICE

Don't lose patience. Let those seasons of wait grow your
endurance. Waiting is hard no matter how you slice
it. We're so impatient, something we all picked up as
children. We want what we want, and we want it now.
And often, we were rewarded for a good ole tantrum.
But as grown women, we're learning that along with
impatience comes stress. With stress comes worry and
fear. So choosing to wait in faith, knowing God's timing is
perfect, is imperative. Let's take a deep breath together
and commit to waiting well, keeping to His path, and
minding His will. Yes, He will come for us.

Why We Can't Fear Man

The fear of man brings a snare, but whoever trusts in and puts his confidence in the LORD will be exalted and safe.

PROVERBS 29:25 AMP

Not only does it cause terrible stress and strain on our heart, but trying to do what we think others want us to do keeps us from being our authentic selves. We simply won't have the confidence to be the woman God intended for us to be. When we're afraid of what others think, it shuts us down or entices us to conform. We'll constantly strive to meet standards others put in place—the ones that change on a whim. And we'll find ourselves trapped on the treadmill of performance, looking for validation and hoping to be loved. But when we activate our faith in God, none of that will matter because we will feel His unexplainable peace through His unmeasurable love.

Choosing Role Models

*Keep your eye on the innocent. Model your
life after the blameless. Everyone who loves
peace has a future. But sinners will be doomed.
The forecast for the wicked: utter destruction.
There will be none left, not one child of darkness.*

PSALM 37:37-38 VOICE

Choose your role models well. Be intentional to follow
people whose lives exemplify Christian living. Keep
your eye on those who walk the walk rather than talk
the talk. There are many out there who look cool
and act carefree, but their hearts are corrupt. They
may act innocent in some circles, but their actions in
others are anything but. Don't be swayed! If you want
to live in peace, surround yourself with others who
live with purpose and passion for the Lord. Let them
encourage you in faith. And even more, be that light
to those around you too.

From the Bottom of Your Heart

Trust GOD from the bottom of your heart; don't try to figure out everything on your own. Listen for GOD's voice in everything you do, everywhere you go; he's the one who will keep you on track.

PROVERBS 3:5–6 MSG

When we try to figure out everything on our own, we worry. We think the mess is ours to fix, so we shut down. Let this scripture be a steadfast reminder to trust God. Go all-in with a heart full of faith, listening for His voice and looking for His way. Without fail, the Lord will keep you on track. God wants the best for your relationships. He wants you to thrive in your calling. His hope is that you stand strong in your convictions. As you trust Him from the bottom of your heart, it will be so.

Just Keep Trusting

While Jesus was still speaking with her,
messengers came from the synagogue leader's
house, saying to Jairus, "Your daughter has died.
Why bother the teacher any longer?" But Jesus
overheard their report and said to the synagogue
leader, "Don't be afraid; just keep trusting."

MARK 5:35-36 CEB

Jesus was challenging Jairus to have radical trust. His daughter had died before Jesus could heal her, but to Him it didn't matter what was happening in the natural. Jesus wanted Jairus to see that too. So often we stress out from what we can see and hear. We focus on only what's happening before our eyes. But the Lord isn't bound by the same laws of nature that we are. That's where faith comes in. Our job is to keep trusting God no matter how things look. Our anxiety will be low. Our fears, manageable. And we'll experience peace in the chaos.

The Act of Running to God and from Evil

Don't assume that you know it all. Run to
GOD! Run from evil! Your body will glow with
health, your very bones will vibrate with
life! Honor GOD with everything you own;
give him the first and the best. Your barns
will burst, your wine vats will brim over.

PROVERBS 3:7-10 MSG

There is an urgency in running toward one thing and away from something else. You can sense a desperation in the coming and going, and it shows a commitment on both sides. When your marriage is in trouble, you run toward it and away from temptation. When you're stuck in unforgiveness, you run toward grace and away from offense. When your finances are a mess, you choose generosity to God over stinginess. And these responses help reduce worry and fear because you experience peace from making the right choice—the honoring choice.

Pushing through Fears

*Because she had heard about Jesus, she came
up behind him in the crowd and touched
his clothes. She was thinking, If I can just
touch his clothes, I'll be healed. Her bleeding
stopped immediately, and she sensed in her
body that her illness had been healed.*

MARK 5:27-29 CEB

This woman had been bleeding for twelve years. She'd
exhausted her resources trying to heal, spending her
last dime on doctors and painful procedures, and the
bleeding continued. The stress of living as an outcast
because of her condition must've been all-consuming.
But she pushed through her fear to find Jesus. All it took
was a touch of His clothes for the bleeding to stop. In
that moment, she was healed. Friend, be bold like this.
Don't let anything keep you from reaching out for the
Lord. Let no amount of apprehension stop you from
pursuing help and healing.

When God Disciplines

But don't, dear friend, resent GOD's discipline;
don't sulk under his loving correction.
It's the child he loves that GOD corrects;
a father's delight is behind all this.
PROVERBS 3:11-12 MSG

No one likes to be disciplined. It never leaves you wanting for more. Instead, it's often frustrating, stressful, and embarrassing. Even when it's of the constructive criticism variety, correction is hard. But we're told to not resent God's discipline since it's done out of His love for us. It's not anger that drives it, but delight. And when we choose to accept it with open arms and an open mind, we will eventually feel a sense of calm. We will have a newfound perspective. Friend, the Lord promises to never leave us in our mess but instead to show us the way out. He is the great Course Corrector, and you can trust it!

95

You Will Have

*I have told you these things, so that in Me you
may have [perfect] peace and confidence.
In the world you have tribulation and trials
and distress and frustration; but be of
good cheer [take courage; be confident,
certain, undaunted]! For I have overcome
the world. [I have deprived it of power to
harm you and have conquered it for you.]*
JOHN 16:33 AMPC

It's so important to understand that we'll face tribulation, trials, distress, and frustrations. Some of our stress comes from *not* knowing that. We feel anxiety when tough situations come, because we assumed God would stop them from happening. But the Word is clear in saying we will face troubles, so grab on to this truth today. At the same time, stand in confidence. The Lord has conquered the world and anything it throws at you. His promise is to save you, heal you, and restore you. With God, your victory is already sealed.

The Need for Wisdom

Wisdom extends to you long life in one
hand and wealth and promotion in the other.
Out of her mouth flows righteousness, and
her words release both law and mercy.
The ways of wisdom are sweet, always
drawing you into the place of wholeness.
PROVERBS 3:16-17 TPT

How does wisdom extend to you a long life? When we are genuine in our desire to make the right choices that honor God, He will bless us. Even when scared and anxious, choosing what is right over what is easy will be rewarded. And when we make the pursuit of wisdom something of value—speaking it, seeking it, seeding it— there will be a sweetness that comes. When you're at a crossroads, stay put until God gives you the next step. Rather than act out of anxiousness, ask for perspective and discernment. It's a step toward wholeness in Him.

The Call to Be Still and Calm

"Be still, be calm, see, and understand I am the True God. I am honored among all the nations. I am honored over all the earth." You know the Eternal, the Commander of heavenly armies, surrounds us and protects us; the True God of Jacob is our shelter, close to His heart.

PSALM 46:10-11 VOICE

For many, being calm and being still are almost impossible, especially when life feels overwhelming. In those times, we jump into overtime and become supersonic, working to fix what's wrong. If we're not in action physically, our minds are racing and our stress is off the charts. But God says there is a better way to handle things, and it starts by understanding He is God and you are not. It means setting aside your plan for His peace. It means being still and calm, trusting you're close to His heart.

Two Goals for Your Life

*My child, never drift off course from these
two goals for your life: to walk in wisdom
and to discover your purpose. Don't ever
forget how they empower you. For they
strengthen you inside and out and inspire
you to do what's right; you will be energized
and refreshed by the healing they bring.*

PROVERBS 3:21-22 TPT

When you walk in wisdom and discover your purpose,
you will feel a new strength coursing through your
veins. These two hand-in-hand goals should be your
north star to godly living. Let them guide your choices
and decisions daily as they inspire you to do the right
thing. When you begin to feel stress or fear creep in,
circle back to make sure these are still your guardrails.
Keeping them in focus will excite you, bring a new energy to living, and offer renewal for your heart.

God Is Closer

God is our shelter and our strength. When troubles seem near, God is nearer, and He's ready to help. So why run and hide? No fear, no pacing, no biting fingernails. When the earth spins out of control, we are sure and fearless. When mountains crumble and the waters run wild, we are sure and fearless.

PSALM 46:1-2 VOICE

Let's rejoice knowing that when trouble is at our doorstep, God is already inside our home. When your child is causing issues at school, or you're having to file bankruptcy, or your marriage is falling apart, remember God is between you and the struggle. He's right there with you, ready to jump in to help. So in every situation that threatens your peace, you can be fearless of the battle because you're sure of the Warrior. He will melt away the stress as you let Him be your shelter and strength.

Confidence in a Crisis

You will not be subject to terror, for it will not terrify you. Nor will the disrespectful be able to push you aside, because God is your confidence in times of crisis, keeping your heart at rest in every situation.

PROVERBS 3:25-26 TPT

When we trust God to give us confidence in a crisis, we won't crumble under the weight of worry. Circumstances might be scary, but He'll keep us from sinking into stress if we steady our eyes on Him. But chances are this isn't how it usually goes. It's not that He isn't ready and waiting, but rather that we don't cry out for help. We put our confidence in our family and friends or ourselves. We rely on worldly solutions and lose our peace. Next time, let God build you up in strength and wisdom so your heart can be at rest no matter what.

One Day

"He will wipe away every tear from their eyes. Death will be no more. There will be no mourning, crying, or pain anymore, for the former things have passed away."

REVELATION 21:4 CEB

What a relief to know that one day we won't live with the kinds of sadness that plague us today. We won't be riddled with bouts of grief from broken relationships. There won't be reasons for mourning because death will be no more. Our hearts will be at peace. We will feel His comfort. And we'll experience rest like never before. Only God can wipe every tear from our eyes, restoring joy to the weary. He's the only One able to remove the worry and fear that knot us up so we can live untangled in freedom. Yes, life can be difficult and painful, but there will come a time when none of that affects us anymore.

The Purpose of Waiting

I pray with great faith for you, because I'm fully convinced that the One who began this gracious work in you will faithfully continue the process of maturing you until the unveiling of our Lord Jesus Christ!

PHILIPPIANS 1:6 TPT

God isn't done with you yet! Go ahead, inhale a deep breath of grace, and exhale the impatience causing anxiety. It's normal to want the Lord to work quickly to finish what He has started. So what are you waiting for? Are you ready to get married? Do you want to start a family? Is the legal process taking too long? Are you struggling to finish your degree? Is the company taking too long to hire? Every waiting period has purpose, and God uses it to mature you in faith. And although you're anxious for closure, trust His perfect timing in each process.

Community Support

*It's no wonder I pray with such confidence, since
you have a permanent place in my heart! You
have remained partners with me in the wonderful
grace of God even though I'm here in chains
for standing up for the truth of the gospel.*
PHILIPPIANS 1:7 TPT

Paul felt community through faith even though he was locked in jail. He prayed confidently because he knew he wasn't alone. What a difference friendship makes in the life of a believer! How has community helped you? Think of the ways they've strengthened your resolve to stand firm as you wait for God's help. Remember the times your heart felt encouraged to forgive an offense because of their perspective and support. Let the people the Lord has put in your life speak truth. Listen as they offer inspired wisdom. Let them hold you up in hard times. And watch as the stress and strife you encounter lose their hold on your life.

Exiles on Earth

*But we are citizens of heaven, exiles on earth
waiting eagerly for a Liberator, our Lord
Jesus the Anointed, to come and transform
these humble, earthly bodies into the form
of His glorious body by the same power
that brings all things under His control.*
PHILIPPIANS 3:20–21 VOICE

What a beautiful revelation to realize we are only exiles on planet Earth. This isn't our home. Our final destination makes our current situation pale in comparison. Friend, relax knowing there won't be any financial struggles to navigate in heaven. We won't face divorce or disease. There won't be reasons for stress about the aging process. Worry about the details of the day will be a thing of the past, and anxiety won't keep us up at night any longer. Soon, our bodies will be transformed as we hang a new welcome sign at the door.

Helped, Not Hindered

I want you to know, dear ones, what has happened to me has not hindered, but helped my ministry of preaching the gospel, causing it to expand and spread to many people. . . . And what I'm going through has actually caused many believers to become even more courageous in the Lord and to be bold and passionate to preach the Word of God, all because of my chains.

PHILIPPIANS 1:12, 14 TPT

While your current season of stress and strife may be wearing on you, God will use it to help others. You may think anxiety-ridden situations have hindered your testimony, but they may be exactly what God will use to spread the Gospel far and wide. The truth is, your faith in tough times encourages others. It emboldens them. And watching you survive and thrive through suffering builds confidence. So, friend, don't hide your hardship, because God will use it.

Checking Your Motives

I am well aware that some people out there are preaching the message of the Anointed One because of jealousies and rivalries. Their motives aren't pure. They're driven by selfish ambitions and personal agendas, hoping somehow to add to my pain here in prison.

PHILIPPIANS 1:15 VOICE

Always be willing to check your motives. There are times we're fully aware we are doing things for all the wrong reasons. Are you trying to look good or sound smart? Are you hoping your family appears to be happy and harmonious? Maybe you want to be revered or seen as an expert. Or maybe you do what you do to look more holy, like your faith is better and stronger than others. The stress comes as you try to keep up the facade, because it takes work! Eventually, the guilt catches up. Just be you—the one God created with delight.

When We Are Paralyzed by Fear

*Don't be paralyzed in any way by what
your opponents are doing. Your steadfast
faith in the face of opposition is a sign
that they are doomed and that you have
been graced with God's salvation.*

PHILIPPIANS 1:28 VOICE

Do you ever find yourself paralyzed by fear? Most do!
Sometimes we're overwhelmed by the situation at hand;
we don't know what to do next. We aren't sure of our
next step, so we freeze up. And we worry we may do
something to worsen the situation, choosing to remain
static instead. Next time, take that fear right to God
and tell Him exactly how you're feeling. Be honest and
open with the One who can effectively strengthen you
and provide insight. This bold decision to be steadfast
won't only reflect your faith but will also keep your feet
firmly planted on the right path.

When You Fear Hidden Traps

*He's the hope that holds me and the stronghold
to shelter me, the only God for me, and my
great confidence. He will rescue you from every
hidden trap of the enemy, and he will protect
you from false accusation and any deadly curse.*

PSALM 91:2-3 TPT

Do you ever worry about the hidden traps of the Enemy?
Maybe you stress thinking your husband may be leading
a secret life. Is there apprehension about saying yes
to a job that seems too good to be true? Maybe you're
waiting for the floor to drop from under you because
things have been so smooth lately. Rather than sink in
hopelessness and fear, look to God for shelter. Expect
Him to rescue you from every trap and trouble. And
let the Lord be your fierce protector no matter the
circumstance you're facing. Never forget you are held.

His Massive Arms

His massive arms are wrapped around you,
protecting you. You can run under his covering
of majesty and hide. His arms of faithfulness
are a shield keeping you from harm.

PSALM 91:4 TPT

Imagine the feeling of safety and love you would experience by being wrapped in God's massive arms. There's something so sweet about that kind of protection, making us feel deeply cherished. You may have some wonderful family and friends who hold you tight in hard times, but nothing or no one can match being nestled by the Creator. What a powerful reason to let Him hug every stress out of us. We should let Him squeeze all the worry and fear away, because being engulfed in His goodness and faithfulness keeps us from harm. So when life is overwhelming and relationships are messy and your self-worth is being assaulted, hide in His embrace and find peace.

You're Joyfully Celebrated

The Eternal your God is standing right here among you, and He is the champion who will rescue you. He will joyfully celebrate over you; He will rest in His love for you; He will joyfully sing because of you like a new husband.

ZEPHANIAH 3:17 VOICE

As women, we have a deep longing to be celebrated. That doesn't mean we want a party or to have our name scrolled on the jumbotron at a stadium. It means we want to be seen and known. Even more, we want those who see us to appreciate us. We want our heart to be recognized. We want our strengths to be acknowledged without our weaknesses being criticized. Friend, don't you know God does this perfectly? He stands with you. He champions you. He rescues you. And the Lord joyfully celebrates you. Let that bring peace to your anxious heart.

When We Need Fresh Strength

But those who wait upon GOD get fresh strength. They spread their wings and soar like eagles, they run and don't get tired, they walk and don't lag behind.

ISAIAH 40:31 MSG

When we're in the middle of a mess, so often what we need the most is a dose of fresh strength. Facing anxiety, we need a boost of motivation so we can continue. Our weary heart and mind crave an infusion of perseverance. We need an injection of endurance so fear doesn't wear us down. And while our human limitations keep us from replenishing ourselves, God most certainly will. At the right time, He'll bring restoration, blessing you with the fortitude to take the next step. Your stamina will help you overcome the stress, and you'll watch in gratitude as things begin to turn around. Always let God be your source.

Running toward the Right Things

Brothers and sisters, as I said, I know I have not arrived; but there's one thing I am doing: I'm leaving my old life behind, putting everything on the line for this mission. I am sprinting toward the only goal that counts: to cross the line, to win the prize, and to hear God's call to resurrection life found exclusively in Jesus the Anointed.

PHILIPPIANS 3:13–14 VOICE

When you began your faith journey, it meant you'd leave your old life behind. It's not always easy, but your change in direction is necessary. Now, your focus is to run toward a righteous life with gusto and not look back. It's going all-in. And when you begin to feel stressed, let it be a red flag you're working in your own strength. This sprint requires God's help and guidance, so make sure He's with you as you run toward the right things.

Your Prayer Is the Trigger

"I will answer your cry for help every time you pray, and you will feel my presence in your time of trouble. I will deliver you and bring you honor. I will satisfy you with a full life and with all that I do for you. For you will enjoy the fullness of my salvation!"

PSALM 91:15-16 TPT

Scripture says God will respond to our cry for help every time we pray. We don't have to say the right words. We don't have to be in the perfect setting. What triggers His action is prayer. Too often, we take on the stress of the day, putting it squarely on our shoulders to handle alone. And right on cue, we end up full of anxiety, fear, and worry. Let God's presence fill you with hope and peace every time life stirs you up. He will deliver you!

When We Need Perspective

Oh Martha, Martha, you are so anxious and concerned about a million details, but really, only one thing matters. Mary has chosen that one thing, and I won't take it away from her.

LUKE 10:41-42 VOICE

Only God can offer the perfect perspective on life. When our focus lands on the wrong things, He is the One who will realign us with truth. Fear and worry may entice us to take our eyes off God, but He will bring us back when we take those things to Him. So ask for insight into your troubled marriage and direction on how to heal it. Let Him bring understanding to your friendship frustrations. Allow God to make you aware of the negative thinking that's draining your joy. Ask Him to sharpen your intuition as you parent. When you let the Lord create and deepen your awareness, anxiety won't have a chance.

Have You Learned to Trust God Yet?

*So they shook him awake, saying, "Teacher,
don't you even care that we are all about to
die!" Fully awake, he rebuked the storm and
shouted to the sea, "Hush! Be still!" All at
once the wind stopped howling and the water
became perfectly calm. Then he turned to his
disciples and said to them, "Why are you so
afraid? Haven't you learned to trust yet?"*

MARK 4:39–40 TPT

Just like Jesus asked the disciples, ask yourself the same
question: During the storm, have you learned to trust
God yet? When you're worried about the interview or
the hard conversation with a friend, how do you handle
it? When the doctor's report confirms your worries, is
your faith activated? In the middle of the misunder-
standing, where is your faith? God is trustworthy at all
times and in every situation facing you. Don't let fear
steal your peace.

Choosing Your Attitude

A joyful, cheerful heart brings healing to both body and soul. But the one whose heart is crushed struggles with sickness and depression.

PROVERBS 17:22 TPT

Your attitude really does make a difference in your heart, and you get to choose what it looks like every day and in each circumstance that comes your way. Even when you're battling stressful moments, you can choose to trust God. Your response of faith will greatly influence how fear impacts your courage and confidence. When insecurities are tangled in a knot, a decision to praise God anyway will transform your mood and usher in peace. So go ahead, let your joy in the Lord shine through every tough situation, and expect Him to show up and shift the atmosphere. Not only will it bless your body, but your soul will soar with optimism no matter what.

You Have a Divine Detail

*God sends angels with special orders to protect
you wherever you go, defending you from all harm.
If you walk into a trap, they'll be there for you
and keep you from stumbling. You'll even walk
unharmed among the fiercest powers of darkness,
trampling every one of them beneath your feet!*

PSALM 91:11-13 TPT

Don't worry, you are fully and completely protected!
You're surrounded by angels on a mission from God to
keep you safe and unharmed. Friend, you are covered.
Did you know you were so loved? Let this truth give you
freedom to follow God's plan for your life, even when
it takes you far out of your comfort zone. Sometimes
we allow fear to keep us stuck. We let insecurity stop
us from moving forward. But understanding you have
a divine detail, be courageous and confident as you
follow God's will for your life.

Keep Your Mouth Shut

"God will fight the battle for you. And you? You keep your mouths shut!"
EXODUS 14:14 MSG

Sometimes the best thing we can do when tensions are high and our heart is heavy is keep our mouth shut. What we really want to do is verbally berate someone out of frustration. Our unease wants to unload. Our worry wants to whack someone over the head. Our stress wants to slip in a statement. But God knows there are certain battles that are His alone. There are times our best option is to let the Lord battle on our behalf while we stay silent. When you feel the Holy Spirit telling you to keep your mouth shut, let it be. Ask God for help to stay hushed. The last thing we want to do is get in His way with our words.

Three Reminders about Temptation

*No test or temptation that comes your way
is beyond the course of what others have
had to face. All you need to remember is that
God will never let you down; he'll never let
you be pushed past your limit; he'll always
be there to help you come through it.*

1 CORINTHIANS 10:13 MSG

Sometimes the tension is palpable from temptation. We feel the stress and fear it brings, often confused with what to do next. But Paul equips us with three powerful reminders. First, remember you won't be disappointed by God because He's incapable of letting you down. Second, the Lord is fully aware of your limitations and won't allow you to be pushed beyond them. And last, He'll help you safely to the other side. God will always be the hero of your story, friend. You are safe when you activate your faith.

Living within the Shadow

When we live our lives within the shadow of God Most High, our secret hiding place, we will always be shielded from harm. How then could evil prevail against us or disease infect us?

PSALM 91:9-10 TPT

This world can sometimes be unsettling. When we take notice of what's happening, fear can rise in our heart. Our unknown future often rattles us to the core. That's why it's imperative to live in God's shadow. Simply put, we allow Him to go before us and we stay safely behind our fierce and protective Father. It's when we step out and take control that we eventually find ourselves stressed and scared. Friend, God is your secret hiding place from the troubles of the world. He's your shield from harm. Don't try to handle things on your own, because it's a one-way ticket to an anxious heart. Stay in His shadow.

God's Love Won't Quit You

Thank GOD because he's good, because his love never quits. Tell the world, Israel, "His love never quits." And you, clan of Aaron, tell the world, "His love never quits." And you who fear GOD, join in, "His love never quits."

PSALM 118:1-4 MSG

We've all felt the sting of rejection. Few things hurt more than having someone walk away from a relationship with you. It tangles every insecurity and whispers, *You're not worthy of love.* Even worse is the amount of time we give to replaying the situation, looking for answers and beating ourselves up. It leaves us stressed out and brokenhearted. Now contrast that with the reality of God's love for you—love that never quits. You never have to worry He will leave you. To the Lord, you are worth every bit of His time and attention. He loves you with an unshakable and unchangeable love.

God Is Your Source of Hope

I pray that God, the source of all hope, will infuse
your lives with an abundance of joy and peace
in the midst of your faith so that your hope will
overflow through the power of the Holy Spirit.

ROMANS 15:13 VOICE

Stress enters your heart when hope fades, and that's why maturing in your faith is so important. We must learn to let God be our source of confidence. We must trust Him to infuse our life with His goodness. Remember: It's a choice to grab hold of joy when things around you are crumbling. And choosing the peace of Jesus so fear and worry don't overtake you requires courage. So, friend, if you're not going to God in prayer every day and asking for His influence over you to reign, you're missing out on the hope a life of faith brings.

When You Feel Pushed to the Wall

Pushed to the wall, I called to GOD; from the wide open spaces, he answered. GOD's now at my side and I'm not afraid; who would dare lay a hand on me? GOD's my strong champion; I flick off my enemies like flies.
PSALM 118:5-7 MSG

What has you pushed to the wall these days? Maybe finances are smothering you. Could it be you're at the end of your rope in waiting? Are your children pushing every button? Maybe you are single, and it feels like time is running out. Maybe you said yes to something and regret it now. Let these stressful situations drive you right to God. He can help you find the breathing room you desperately need. He can replace your fears with courage. He can rebuild your confidence, giving you wisdom on what to do next. Let God be your champion.

You Need the Lord

Jesus looked hard at them and said, "No chance at all if you think you can pull it off yourself. Every chance in the world if you trust God to do it."
MATTHEW 19:26 MSG

As much as we may try in our pride and determination, we cannot make it through this life without God. We need His constant companionship to help us navigate the hard moments when our heart is broken. We need His wisdom when we come to a fork in the road. As life gets chaotic, we need the Lord to bring a sense of calm so we can see clearly. God is the One who steadies us when our anxiety is off the charts. And it's important to change our mindset and accept that our best hope for a life lived well is the Lord. Grab hold of Him and never let go.

Take Refuge in God Alone

Far better to take refuge in GOD than trust in people; far better to take refuge in GOD than trust in celebrities.

PSALM 118:8-9 MSG

Don't be misled to trust anyone or anything other than God, because there will be countless opportunities that come your way with big assurances in tow. Some will look to be a sure thing, but they are nothing more than empty promises. Others will be familiar fixes we always seem to come back to. We are creatures of habit and comfort, that's for sure. And every one of these will cause our heart to be anxious once they fail us again. We are imperfect people living in an imperfect world with imperfect solutions. But when you let the Lord be your refuge above all else, you'll find a sense of peace that lasts.

When You Don't Know Why

LORD, you have examined me. You know me.
You know when I sit down and when I stand up.
Even from far away, you comprehend my plans.
You study my traveling and resting.
You are thoroughly familiar with all my ways.

PSALM 139:1-3 CEB

If God is so familiar with you, your thoughts and your habits, trust Him to get to the bottom of what's stressing you out. Most of the time, we know what's bothering us. We can point to the situation, the person, or the season with ease. But other times, we're living with an underlying sense of anxiety we can't put our finger on. We feel it, but we don't know why. Let God be the One you go to for clarity. Let Him reveal what's stirring you up. Without a doubt, He knows, and when you ask, He will open your eyes to understanding.

On the Edge

I was right on the cliff-edge, ready to fall, when
GOD grabbed and held me. GOD's my strength,
he's also my song, and now he's my salvation.
Hear the shouts, hear the triumph songs in
the camp of the saved? "The hand of GOD has
turned the tide! The hand of GOD is raised in
victory! The hand of GOD has turned the tide!"

PSALM 118:14–16 MSG

Think back to a time when you were on the edge—a time when you wanted to give up and be done. Was it after a hard work week? Were you fighting back from a health struggle? Maybe you were battling addiction. Maybe the relationship was too broken to fix. These are times we need God to hold us tight. It's when we need His supernatural strength and wisdom. And it's His hand that'll turn the tide and replenish our grit to go on.

You're Never Alone

*There isn't a word on my tongue, LORD, that you
don't already know completely. You surround
me—front and back. You put your hand on me.
That kind of knowledge is too much for me;
it's so high above me that I can't reach it.*

PSALM 139:4-6 CEB

Few things feel worse than loneliness. Sitting at home
without options makes us feel lousy. We waste so much
time complaining that no one wants to know us or hang
out with us that we forget what God thinks. The reality
is there may be few on earth that make the effort, but
the Lord already knows every word you will speak. His
love surrounds you because you're worthy of knowing.
And when you really think about it, be awestruck by how
profoundly you're loved and how valuable you are to
Him. Regardless of how it may feel, you're never alone.

The Day Is God's

This is the very day of the Lord that brings
gladness and joy, filling our hearts with glee.
O God, please come and save us again;
bring us your breakthrough-victory!
PSALM 118:24-25 TPT

Where are you in need of God's breakthrough-victory right now? Maybe you are struggling to forgive an offense. Are you working through grief and loss? Is the adjustment of being newly single again hard to navigate? Maybe you're afraid of stepping out of your comfort zone in ministry or you are lacking courage to branch out in your career. These are the kinds of things that keep us from gladness and joy. They can keep us stuck. But the psalmist reminds us that today is God's, and He will bring gladness and joy if we ask. He will fill us with happiness! We can be joyful as we wait for breakthrough.

Can't Get Away from His Love

Where could I go to get away from your spirit?
Where could I go to escape your presence?
If I went up to heaven, you would be there. If I
went down to the grave, you would be there too!
PSALM 139:7-8 CEB

No matter how much you mess up, it will never be enough to remove you from God's compassion and love. Even when you're careless with your words or impulsive with your actions, you can't hide from Him. You are seen and known to the core by the Father who adores you. So release the worry that says God will leave you. It's not possible. Undo the straps of stress that whisper His love is conditional. It's not true. There's no place you can go to escape Him. Because He loves you with such fervor, He will always be with you.

You're Marvelous

You are the one who created my innermost parts; you knit me together while I was still in my mother's womb. I give thanks to you that I was marvelously set apart. Your works are wonderful—I know that very well.

PSALM 139:13-14 CEB

Friend, you are made marvelously. How does that truth sit in your spirit? For some, it stirs up wounds from times we were told the opposite. We wince thinking it could be reality. It embarrasses us because we feel anything but marvelous. And it makes us anxious, confused on how to respond to a statement that feels so profound. It's difficult to have confidence in it. Honestly, it takes grit and guts to believe we are God's wonderful creation. Ask the Lord to graft this truth into your heart. Ask Him to replace with His truth the lies you've believed for so long. It may take time, but He'll do it.

Root of Anxiety

God, I invite your searching gaze into my heart.
Examine me through and through; find out
everything that may be hidden within me. Put me
to the test and sift through all my anxious cares.
See if there is any path of pain I'm walking on,
and lead me back to your glorious, everlasting
way—the path that brings me back to you.

PSALM 139:23-24 TPT

When you feel anxious but aren't sure why, ask God to reveal the root. Let Him examine your heart to know why you're stirred up. Sometimes we aren't aware of underlying worries. There's a foreboding we can't shake. And in our confusion and fear, we aren't always kind to those trying to support us. When we leave the revealing and healing to God, asking Him to sift through every apprehension, He'll get to the source. The Lord is the One who will restore peace.

That Sense of Dread

"You will hear of wars and revolutions on every side, with more rumors of wars to come. Don't panic or give in to your fears, for the breaking apart of the world's systems is destined to happen. But it won't yet be the end; it will still be unfolding."

MATTHEW 24:6 TPT

With the state of the nation and world, you may feel a sense of dread. You might worry about how your kids or aging parents will cope with change. It doesn't look as if things will get any better, and we may lack hope that they will. Friend, God is your source of peace in this season of life. Take every stress and fear directly to Him. Scriptures tell us the world isn't falling apart but rather into place. The stage is being set for Jesus to come back. So let God give you peace and perspective every day.

This Is Who You Are

Remember: you're a people set apart for the Eternal your God; He is your God and has chosen you to be His own possession—His special people—out of all the peoples on the earth. The Eternal didn't become devoted to you and choose you because you were the most numerous of all the peoples—in fact, you were the least!

DEUTERONOMY 7:6-7 VOICE

When you're feeling insignificant, revisit today's scripture to be reminded of who you are. It's important to take those worries to the Word of God because it offers a powerful perspective on the insecurities you're feeling. And your anxious heart will find peace in its truths! Did you know you're set apart by God? He chose you, friend. You are special and important. And it's because of who you are—not what you do, what you look like, or what you have—that you're chosen.

Weigh and Examine

*My dear friends, don't believe everything
you hear. Carefully weigh and examine what
people tell you. Not everyone who talks
about God comes from God. There are a lot
of lying preachers loose in the world.*

1 JOHN 4:1 MSG

Have you ever heard someone describe God or the Christian life and you immediately felt tension from their words? Something didn't sit right in your spirit, and it made you feel uneasy. Listen to that prompting, and follow up by opening the Word of God. Because we know it to be truth, anything that goes against the Bible is heresy. It's vital we always weigh and examine what others say so we don't adopt the wrong doctrine. And that stirring in your gut is often the Holy Spirit warning you, so be sensitive to it and ask God for clarification. He will bring peace and truth.

He Is the Faithful God

I want you to know that the Eternal your God is the only true God. He's the faithful God who keeps His covenants and shows loyal love for a thousand generations to those who in return love Him and keep His commands.

DEUTERONOMY 7:9 VOICE

One way you can live a less stressed life is to remember that God is faithful to the promises He has made—both those from His Word and those whispered into your spirit. Because the Lord has vowed to bring hope and healing, nothing can stop it. Since He pledges peace, it will come in spades when you ask for it. As God has assured strength for the battle, wisdom for the decision, and restoration for the broken, it will come to be. So knowing He is faithful, let it keep stress and fear at bay.

Gotta Love Them All

Those who say, "I love God" and hate their brothers or sisters are liars. After all, those who don't love their brothers or sisters whom they have seen can hardly love God whom they have not seen! This commandment we have from him: Those who claim to love God ought to love their brother and sister also.

1 JOHN 4:20-21 CEB

Today's scripture sets us straight on what love is and is not. It challenges us to look at our heart and requires us to love with intention. We simply cannot love God while we hate others. He's commanded us to love those who are hard to love. Maybe it's a petty ex-husband or a cranky aunt. Maybe it's a mean coworker or a nosey neighbor. It may even be a child who treats you like trash. Ask God to help you love them, and it will help heal your anxious heart toward them.

Asking in Agreement

This is the confidence that we have in our relationship with God: If we ask for anything in agreement with his will, he listens to us. If we know that he listens to whatever we ask, we know that we have received what we asked from him.
1 JOHN 5:14-15 CEB

Asking for something in agreement with God's will means your heart is in alignment with His. Chances are that doesn't include a brand-new, souped-up car; a bigger house in a gated community; or more followers on Facebook. But if your request is for confidence to step out of your comfort zone to follow God's lead, He'll grant it. If you want to love the unlovable and forgive the unforgivable, it will come. If you need peace to replace anxiety or courage to replace fear, it will be yours. God hears you and will bless you!

Rescued from the World

He's the Anointed One who offered himself as the sacrifice for our sins! He has rescued us from this evil world system and set us free, just as our Father God desired.

GALATIANS 1:4 TPT

This world has a way of stressing us out because we wonder how the ups and downs will negatively affect us. Will I be able to afford rising costs? Will my job be stable in a changing economy? Will I have to downsize to make ends meet? This can be a challenging place for us, especially because evil is prevalent. And it's exactly why we need to set our heart and mind on things above. We need to focus on the Lord and His promises because Jesus' death rescued us, solidifying a home for us in heaven. Keep a healthy perspective on the world's limitations by trusting a limitless God.

We Must Guard

*So be careful. Guard your hearts. They
can be made heavy with moral laxity, with
drunkenness, with the hassles of daily life.
Then the day I've been telling you about might
catch you unaware and trap you. Because
it's coming—nobody on earth will escape it.*

LUKE 21:34-35 VOICE

Scripture says when we don't guard our heart from the
ways of the world, it weighs us down with worry. The
tension overwhelms our peaceful heart, keeping us from
watching for the return of Jesus. So how do we protect
our heart? We don't allow the world to choose how we
live. We follow the path of peace, making choices that
align with God's will. We know what the Bible says, so
we can discern what is right and what is wrong. And
we choose to live each day expecting His return, intentionally living and loving well.

Watered Down

I'm obviously not trying to flatter you or water
down my message to be popular with men,
but my supreme passion is to please God.
For if all I attempt to do is please people,
I would fail to be a true servant of Christ.
GALATIANS 1:10 TPT

Go ahead and be bold when you speak truth. You can share with passion and still honor the listener. You can be honest and still show love and respect. It may be challenging, but with the Lord, you can do hard things. The rub comes when we water down our message out of fear of what others might think. When we let worry convince us to leave out parts that may be unpopular or uncompromising, it doesn't please God. Pray first, asking for the right words. Ask Him to prepare the listener's heart. Then say what needs to be said with God-given confidence.

Don't Plan Your Words

This will be your opportunity—your opportunity to tell your story. Make up your mind in advance not to plan your strategy for answering their questions, for when the time comes, I will give you the words to say— wise words—which none of your adversaries will be able to answer or argue against.

LUKE 21:13-15 VOICE

Many of us plan ahead because it helps alleviate stress. Maybe it's self-preservation, because we don't want to look silly. Maybe it's pride, because we don't want to sound dumb. Or maybe it's a lack of trust that God will give us the right words. Regardless, it's a source of anxiety we want to avoid. But what if we took the leap of faith and trusted Him. If God says He'll give words then He will. Still, prep and do research. Have an idea of direction. But let God lead.

Battling a Reputation

The only thing they heard about me was this: "Our former enemy, who once brutally persecuted us, is now preaching the good news of the faith that he tried to destroy!" Because of the transformation that took place in my life, they praised God even more!

GALATIANS 1:23-24 TPT

Just like Paul, you may be battling a former life. Your reputation may be stuck in the past, unable to catch up to the transformation made. And it may be stressful to continually battle the old. Friend, let God bring comfort to your anxious heart as He reminds you to trust His will and ways. It may be that He wants the contrast to be an encouragement to others. There is always a higher purpose. So rather than stress, stand. Instead of worrying, wait. And trust Him with your reputation.

Still in the Miracle Business

When they all saw him walking on the waves,
they thought he was a ghost and screamed out
in terror. But he said to them at once, "Don't yield
to fear. Have courage. It's really me—I Am!"

MARK 6:49-50 TPT

The disciples were freaked out when they saw the awesomeness of Jesus walking on the water. They had seen miracles from Him before. They spent time with Jesus, so they knew of His wonderful ways. They'd listened to His powerful teaching. But they never expected Him to walk on water. The Lord is still in the miracle business today, so be expectant and ready for Him to intervene in your stress-filled situation and bring deliverance. It may not be in the ways you prayed for, but God will bring help and healing in His ways. So have courage! Don't yield to fear! And keep your eyes open.

Peace for the Calling

Jesus, undeterred, went right ahead and gave his charge: "God authorized and commanded me to commission you: Go out and train everyone you meet, far and near, in this way of life, marking them by baptism in the threefold name: Father, Son, and Holy Spirit. Then instruct them in the practice of all I have commanded you. I'll be with you as you do this, day after day after day, right up to the end of the age."

MATTHEW 28:18-20 MSG

Your heart will be at peace when you embrace His call on your life. It may be out of your comfort zone, but when your life aligns with God's will, it's powerful. If there's overwhelming anxiety, the Lord will help you find peace. He will calm your heart. So don't let apprehension be a reason to walk away from what God has designed you to do. He's with you every step of the way!

Infused with His Strength

On the day I needed You, I called, and You responded and infused my soul with strength.
PSALM 138:3 VOICE

Think of the stress and anxiety we could avoid if our souls were infused with God's strength. Our fear often comes when we're at the end of ourselves. When we feel weak in our resolve to love our husbands with more passion and purpose, we lose hope. Every time we get to the end of our rope with our kids, we're worried they'll pay for our inadequacies. Because we lack the energy to work out friendship issues, we're afraid of ending up alone. Our human condition limits every area of life, which is why we need the Lord so desperately. So let God know the burdens of your heart, and ask Him to infuse you with His strength. You don't have to handle everything on your own.

God's Name and Word Are Over It

To You, Lord, I give my whole heart, a heart filled
with praise, for I am grateful; before the gods,
my heart sings praises to You and You alone.
I bow before You, looking to Your holy temple,
and praise Your name, for Your unfailing love
and Your truth; for You have placed Your name
and Your word over all things and all times.
PSALM 138:1-2 VOICE

When God places His name and Word over all things and all times, it means He is above your stress and strife. Every worrisome circumstance has been trumped. Relationships causing concern are under God's eye. Fear of the future, anxiety in the present, or apprehension from the past fall under the blood of Jesus. Let that usher in peace for your heart today. Your heavenly Father's name and Word are over it all. You'll be okay.

Freedom to Take Chances

*Whenever I walk into trouble, You are there
to bring me out. You hold out Your hand to
protect me against the wrath of my enemies,
and hold me safely in Your right hand.*
PSALM 138:7 VOICE

You can live a less stressed life by realizing God will always be there to bring you out of trouble. You may get yourself into a bind, but you're not stuck for good. Enemies may surround you, but there will be a path out with God's help. Your Father in heaven will always keep watch over you, making sure you're safe and secure. And when you choose to grab on to that powerful truth, it will reduce your anxiety levels because you'll know you're covered. It will give you the freedom to take chances and try new things. So trust God and let your confidence grow bigger than any fear.

God's Ability to Multitask

They will marvel at the Eternal's ways,
and they will sing, for great is the glory of
the Eternal. Although He is greatest of all,
He is attentive to the needy and keeps His
distance from the proud and pompous.
PSALM 138:5–6 VOICE

Sometimes we think God is busier with bigger issues than the little ones we're facing. We think our marriage stresses are nothing compared to problems in the Middle East. We decide our financial worries don't hold a candle to the poverty issues facing so many in the world. And why ask for confidence as you parent a headstrong child when you're certain God is focused on greater things. But there is no limit to God's ability to multitask, and He always wants to hear your heart. He's never too busy to care about and act on what burdens you. He can handle it all, and He wants to.

God Will Finish

The Eternal will finish what He started in me.
Your faithful love, O Eternal One, lasts forever;
do not give up on what Your hands have made.

PSALM 138:8 VOICE

Don't you worry, you haven't ruined anything. Yes, maybe you made a bad decision in your parenting. Maybe you didn't follow through at work. Maybe you've been careless in protecting your marriage. And maybe you've walked away from the faith, choosing your own way over God's. But the Word is clear when it says the Lord will finish what He has started in you. That's a guarantee you can't mess it up for good because you simply don't have that kind of power. You may cause a lengthy delay or a messy detour, but God isn't finished with you yet. You can't derail His plans. So take a deep breath, friend, and then turn back to the Lord. He's ready.

God's Mercy and Grace

*Please, God, show me mercy! Open your grace-
fountain for me, for you are my soul's true
shelter. I will hide beneath the shadow of your
embrace, under the wings of your cherubim,
until this terrible trouble is past. I will cry out to
you, the God of the highest heaven, the mighty
God, who performs all these wonders for me.*

PSALM 57:1-2 TPT

When the revelation of what we've done settles, we're often overwhelmed with grief. We are overcome by shame and guilt, saddened by our choices. Our heart is anxious, and we beat ourselves up for doing what we know was offensive. And while we may want to hide instead, the very best thing we can do in these times is run to God. Let Him bring peace. Let Him wipe the tears. And let the Lord restore us through His grace and mercy. There really is no other option.

The Problem with a Father's Love

*From heaven he will send a father's help to
save me. He will trample down those who
trample me.... He will always show me
love by his gracious and constant care.*

PSALM 57:3 TPT

How does it feel to know God will send a *father's* help
for you? Honestly, for many of us, our fathers were
anything but a source of safety and joy. They provided
more stress than security. Their love felt absent or
conditional. And maybe you don't look back on your
childhood fondly because it's too painful. But your
Father in heaven isn't the same as your earthly one.
He loves perfectly, protects perfectly, and is full of
grace and compassion. Let Him be the kind of dad you
need, one who will love you fiercely, consistently, and
without fail. Let Him redefine the word *father* in your
troubled heart.

A Quiet and Confident Heart

My heart, O God, is quiet and confident.
Now I can sing with passion your wonderful
praises! Awake, O my soul, with the music of
his splendor-song! Arise, my soul, and sing his
praises! My worship will awaken the dawn,
greeting the daybreak with my songs of praise!

PSALM 57:7-8 TPT

What would need to happen for your heart to be quiet and confident? With so many distractions and agitations coming at us every day, it's difficult to find peace. Sometimes the chaos feels too overwhelming, like we're always playing catch-up. But scripture confirms it is possible to find a sense of calm and assuredness through our praise. Taking the time to recognize God's goodness settles your soul and puts your eyes on Him rather than on the stressors of the day. And it refocuses you from worry to the wonders of the Lord.

When We Crave Extravagance

Your love is so extravagant it reaches to the heavens; your faithfulness so astonishing it stretches to the sky! Lord God, be exalted as you soar throughout the heavens. May your shining glory be shown in the skies! Let it be seen high above all the earth!

PSALM 57:10-11 TPT

As women, our hearts long to experience extravagant love. We want to be adored and cherished. We want to be understood and valued for our thoughts and ideas. And when those desires constantly elude us, our heart becomes heavy with hopelessness. But that's why it's vital we remember that what we can't find here on earth, we most certainly can find through our heavenly Father. Without fail, God loves you in excess. He is overgenerous in His adoration. And His faithfulness is unmatched. So let your anxious heart rest, because your desire for extravagance is met.

God Will Grant You Peace

The LORD bless you and protect you.
The LORD make his face shine on you and
be gracious to you. The LORD lift up his
face to you and grant you peace.
NUMBERS 6:24-26 CEB

When you begin to feel stressed out, revisit this verse. Read it out loud in first person, personalizing it for yourself when you need it most. Remember, there is power in the Word of God, and the scriptures can bring peace and healing to your anxious heart. There is no reason to battle alone, especially when we have a loving Father who is ready to help. We are desperate for peace, giving us what we need to thrive rather than just survive. So be quick to open God's Word or say a prayer. He knows exactly what you need in the moment, and it will be given.

Nothing Is Impossible with God

*"Not one promise from God is empty of
power. Nothing is impossible with God!"*
LUKE 1:37 TPT

These beautiful words were uttered by the archangel
Gabriel as he told Mary she was to be mother to Jesus,
the Savior of the world. He also revealed that her much
older aunt was already with child, a feat impossible
at her age. These pregnancies were nothing short of
miracles, a chance for God to showcase His majesty.
Friend, let their stories encourage your current reality
and give you hope that good things are in store for you
too. Even when the marriage seems irreparable, God
can restore it. When your finances are in shambles,
God can fix it. When your broken heart is unable to
trust, God can put it back together again. Nothing is
impossible with the Lord, so don't stress out.

God Doesn't Hide from You

"At that time, you will call out for Me, and I will hear. You will pray, and I will listen. You will look for Me intently, and you will find Me."
JEREMIAH 29:12-13 VOICE

What a gift to know the Lord doesn't hide from us. Each time we cry out in strife or stress, our voice is heard. When fear-laced tears run down our face in those private moments, God sees and collects them all. As we drop to our knees in surrender, releasing every burden at His feet, know He's listening with great intention. Don't ever believe the lie that says God is unavailable or uninterested. He isn't keeping His distance from you. And when you realize how much He craves a deeper relationship because you delight His heart, it will create confidence to recognize God as your source. He alone will bring peace to your heart.

Deep Roots of Faith

"But blessed is the man who trusts me, GOD,
the woman who sticks with GOD. They're
like trees replanted in Eden, putting down
roots near the rivers—never a worry through
the hottest of summers, never dropping a
leaf, serene and calm through droughts,
bearing fresh fruit every season."

JEREMIAH 17:7-8 MSG

Today's verse is a lifeline when we're stirred up and battling feelings of anxiety. It reminds us that the key to a less stressed life is choosing to trust God. It matters when we stick with the Lord regardless of the storm we're in. Friend, when you decide to press into God for help and hope, it deepens your roots and anchors your faith. And it's that depth of trust that keeps you calm whether your life is facing a drought or a flood. It keeps you steady and secure.

Compassion Fatigue

*So let's not allow ourselves to get fatigued
doing good. At the right time we will harvest
a good crop if we don't give up, or quit. Right
now, therefore, every time we get the chance, let
us work for the benefit of all, starting with the
people closest to us in the community of faith.*

GALATIANS 6:9–10 MSG

Don't let yourself get weary as you do good things. So
often, that's easier said than done because we get compassion fatigue. We tire of being the one to handle it
all. We become bitter that we always must lace up our
shoes and do the right things. And we may even struggle
with motives, doing good works because we're hoping
to impress someone else. These unsettled feelings can
fill us with anxiousness. Friend, we need God's help
to walk this out well. Tap into the Lord for strength,
motivation, and perseverance.

God Won't Let You Go

"I am Yahweh, your mighty God! I grip your right hand and won't let you go! I whisper to you: 'Don't be afraid; I am here to help you!'"
ISAIAH 41:13 TPT

Sometimes we just want someone to hold our hand and tell us everything will be okay. We want to be held and hugged until our courage returns. We need to hear words of encouragement so anxiety doesn't get the best of us. We need to know we're not alone in the battle for peace. So when you are struggling in relationships, worried about parenting decisions, overwhelmed by a doctor's report, or scared how things will turn out, remember God is mighty. There is none above Him. He has no equal. And the Lord knows exactly what you need to settle your spirit. He won't ever let you go.

Don't Let Stress Win

Live creatively, friends. If someone falls into sin, forgivingly restore him, saving your critical comments for yourself. You might be needing forgiveness before the day's out. Stoop down and reach out to those who are oppressed. Share their burdens, and so complete Christ's law. If you think you are too good for that, you are badly deceived.

GALATIANS 6:1-3 MSG

When you live and love well, it's hard to be full of anxiety. It's difficult to be mean-spirited and loving at the same time. You can't be stressed out and full of compassion because they can't coexist in your heart. Instead, give your worrisome fears to the Lord so you can be freed to be a blessing to those around you. Reach out to those who need it. Restore the broken. Share the burdens others carry. You can't be a light when stress is winning.

How to Live a Stressful Life

*Make a careful exploration of who you are
and the work you have been given, and then
sink yourself into that. Don't be impressed with
yourself. Don't compare yourself with others.
Each of you must take responsibility for doing
the creative best you can with your own life.*

GALATIANS 6:4–5 MSG

If you want to live a stressful life, go ahead and compare yourself to others. Match their very best efforts with the areas in which you struggle. Look at the places they excel in work and life, and see where you can't measure up. Don't consider that you are different people with different talents. Don't consider how uneven the playing field may be. And be predisposed to thinking of yourself as worthless anyway. Ignore what makes you amazing. Yes, this is a guaranteed plan to foster anxiety. Don't do it.

Keeping Our Eyes on God

"Do not yield to fear, for I am always near.
Never turn your gaze from me, for I am your
faithful God. I will infuse you with my strength
and help you in every situation. I will hold
you firmly with my victorious right hand."

ISAIAH 41:10 TPT

When we take our eyes off God and stare at the scary circumstances we're trying to navigate, stress is inevitable. We're choosing to stop trusting the Lord, placing the burden of handling things on our own shoulders. In the end, we will give in to the fear and give up on finding a solution. What a shame to turn our back on the only One who can strengthen and guide us in every situation. God is right here, waiting to steady you and bring deliverance. He will keep you from destruction if you let Him.

What Are You Planting?

Don't be misled: No one makes a fool of God. What a person plants, he will harvest. The person who plants selfishness, ignoring the needs of others—ignoring God!—harvests a crop of weeds. All he'll have to show for his life is weeds! But the one who plants in response to God, letting God's Spirit do the growth work in him, harvests a crop of real life, eternal life.

GALATIANS 6:7-8 MSG

What a great reminder to be intentional in what we plant in our life. If we worry and stress all day long, our harvest won't be full of goodness. If we plant anxiety in our heart and let fear drive every decision we face, our crop will be fruitless. The opposite is also true. If we choose to plant seeds of trust and faith in the Lord, our crop will flourish and lead us into eternal life in heaven.

When We Stress Over Basic Needs

*"I, Yahweh, will respond to the cry of the
poor and needy when they are thirsty and
their tongues are parched with thirst! When
they seek a drink of water but there is none,
I, the God of Israel, will not abandon them."*
ISAIAH 41:17 TPT

When we are worried about having our basic needs
met, that kind of fear can be overwhelming and desta-
bilizing. If we add into the mix our concern for family,
uncertain how they will get what they need to thrive,
it's often too much for our anxious heart to handle. This
is where we must dig in with our faith and trust God.
We must know—because the Bible tells us again and
again—that He not only sees the need but will provide.
Fear and stress make us doubt, so ask the Lord to bring
hope and help. . .and He will.

Fresh Words That Build Up

Don't let even one rotten word seep out of your mouths. Instead, offer only fresh words that build others up when they need it most. That way your good words will communicate grace to those who hear them.

EPHESIANS 4:29 VOICE

When we're stressed out, the words we use often reflect it. Some may spew cuss words to anyone who will listen. Some may take out their frustration by verbally berating others. And some may use their own words to beat themselves up. Anxiety often causes us to act in ways we normally wouldn't. But what if instead we chose to use fresh words that would build up and encourage? What if rather than use rotten words as by-products of stress, we measured them, allowing only kind and generous words to flow from our mouths. What a blessing it would be to everyone, including you.

It's Because You Are Chosen

"I drew you to myself from the ends of the earth and called you from its farthest corner. I say to you: 'You are my servant; I have chosen you. I have not rejected you!'"

ISAIAH 41:9 TPT

There are times it may be hard to imagine that you are good enough for God Almighty to call out your name. Maybe it's even harder to believe He saw value in you and chose to draw you close. In our imperfection and rebellion, we know the things we've done to grieve His heart. We remember the times we chose to walk away and do what we wanted instead of following His lead. But God doesn't love you for the things you've done. Your value doesn't come from the words you speak. He loves you because He chose you. Let that powerful truth bring peace into your anxious heart today.

Ready to Overwhelm You

God is ready to overwhelm you with more blessings than you could ever imagine so that you'll always be taken care of in every way and you'll have more than enough to share.
2 CORINTHIANS 9:8 VOICE

Relax and take a deep breath. You've been battling the fear that things may not work out for a while now. You have been worried about finances, unsure you can make ends meet. And in your anxious moments, you have felt suffocated at times because the outcomes and endings feel tragic. Too often, the stress gets worse because we don't involve God. Scripture says He is ready to overwhelm you with abundance—having more than enough to share with others. He wants to bless you beyond what you thought possible. And when you trust God to help, that choice will restore the peace that's missing in your heart.

Living and Loving Well

As a prisoner of the Lord, I urge you:
Live a life that is worthy of the calling He
has graciously extended to you. Be humble.
Be gentle. Be patient. Tolerate one another in
an atmosphere thick with love. Make every effort
to preserve the unity the Spirit has already
created, with peace binding you together.

EPHESIANS 4:1-3 VOICE

If you are filled with stress, how will you be able to effectively love others? When you're worried, it's difficult to also be humble, gentle, and patient. Preserving an atmosphere of unity is hard when you're absorbed with fear. And peace can't bind you with others when you are full of anxiety. With God's help, you can live and love well. You can choose to walk out the calling on your life with purpose. And peace will reign in your heart as you focus on your relationship with the Father.

Giving from a Peaceful Heart

*But I will say this to encourage your generosity:
the one who plants little harvests little, and
the one who plants plenty harvests plenty.
Giving grows out of the heart—otherwise,
you've reluctantly grumbled "yes" because you
felt you had to or because you couldn't say
"no," but this isn't the way God wants it. For
we know that "God loves a cheerful giver."*

2 CORINTHIANS 9:6-7 VOICE

When you're worried about money, the Bible says to be generous, citing the concept of sowing and reaping. Because God wants us to be cheerful givers, it's important to have the right attitude and motives. When we feel roped into giving, we will do so grudgingly. We may give so we look holy or feel better or to try to manipulate God's blessing. But giving should come from a peaceful heart not an anxious one.

The Old versus the New

Then you know to take off your former way of life, your crumpled old self—that dark blot of a soul corrupted by deceitful desire and lust— to take a fresh breath and to let God renew your attitude and spirit. Then you are ready to put on your new self, modeled after the very likeness of God: truthful, righteous, and holy.
EPHESIANS 4:22-24 VOICE

There is a stress that often occurs naturally as we battle the transition from the old self to the new self. We want to fully embrace the beautiful change that comes from choosing faith, but the pull to return to what's familiar is hard to pass up at times. And the tension between the two stirs up anxiety in our heart. If we ask, God will renew our attitude and spirit so we can find the courage to choose freedom once and for all.

The Stress of Weakness

*So I'm not defeated by my weakness, but delighted!
For when I feel my weakness and endure
mistreatment—when I'm surrounded with troubles
on every side and face persecution because of
my love for Christ—I am made yet stronger. For
my weakness becomes a portal to God's power.*
2 CORINTHIANS 12:10 TPT

Don't let your weaknesses stress you out. They aren't your identity, and we all fall short of the glory of God. Amen? Maybe you struggle most in relationships, having a hard time trusting others. Maybe you clam up rather than speak up for yourself or others. Maybe you are impulsive and tend to make decisions without first thinking through them. Look at these as opportunities for God's strength to shine through you. Every time you feel surrounded by trouble and at the end of your rope, ask the Lord to infuse you with His power.

The Problem with Anger

So put away your lies and speak the truth to one another because we are all part of one another. When you are angry, don't let it carry you into sin. Don't let the sun set with anger in your heart or give the devil room to work.

EPHESIANS 4:25-27 VOICE

Anger is a tough one to navigate at times. Even if justified, we often let it disrupt our peace. God knew anger could carry us into sin if we let it take hold; therefore, we should not let it fester over days. Doing so allows the devil a stronghold. And when anger takes root, along with it comes stress and fear, as well as a nasty sense of justification that keeps it alive inside. Because God wants us to live in peace, we must extend forgiveness quickly so our hearts don't stay stirred up.

Feeling Intimidated

*Then Moses summoned Joshua. He said to him
with all Israel watching, "Be strong. Take courage.
You will enter the land with this people, this land
that GOD promised their ancestors that he'd give
them. You will make them the proud possessors
of it. GOD is striding ahead of you. He's right
there with you. He won't let you down; he won't
leave you. Don't be intimidated. Don't worry."*

DEUTERONOMY 31:7-8 MSG

Imagine the intimidation Joshua must have felt knowing he was to fill Moses' shoes. Replacing someone so respected by man and loved by God may have felt overwhelming at best. But the Bible records countless times he's told to be strong and courageous. And in the end, Joshua did what God had planned. Let this encourage you to stand firm in what intimidates you. When you let the Lord lead and empower you, you'll be unstoppable in the face of hard things.

Calling You Higher

Banish bitterness, rage and anger, shouting and slander, and any and all malicious thoughts—these are poison. Instead, be kind and compassionate. Graciously forgive one another just as God has forgiven you through the Anointed, our Liberating King.

EPHESIANS 4:31-32 VOICE

The only thing bitterness, rage, anger, shouting, and slander will do for you is create stressful living. It will keep your emotions stirred up and unsettled. Hateful thoughts will do nothing but fuel anxious thoughts. And when you find yourself stuck in a cycle of mean-spiritedness, it will rob every bit of peace from you. Let this verse call you higher by challenging you to live differently. Why not decide to be kind and compassionate instead? Choose to extend grace and forgive just like God has forgiven you. When you embrace this kind of living, you'll experience harmony in your heart that can't be matched.

The Purpose of the Thorn

The extraordinary level of the revelations I've received is no reason for anyone to exalt me. For this is why a thorn in my flesh was given to me, the Adversary's messenger sent to harass me, keeping me from becoming arrogant. Three times I pleaded with the Lord to relieve me of this.

2 CORINTHIANS 12:7-8 TPT

Even Paul had a thorn that God chose to not remove because He used it for a good reason. Paul could have allowed it to be a huge cause for anxiety, but he did not. It could have been a reason to complain and whine, but Paul didn't take that route either. And even though he begged God to remove it with no relief, he recognized its divine purpose to keep him humble. Maybe rather than protest about your own thorn, choose to believe God has reason for it. Instead of stressing, trust.

The Stress from Making Decisions

The way you counsel me makes me praise you more, for your whispers in the night give me wisdom, showing me what to do next. Because I set you, Yahweh, always close to me, my confidence will never be weakened, for I experience your wraparound presence every moment.

PSALM 16:7-8 TPT

Think of all the stress that comes from having to make decisions. We worry that we'll make the wrong one and we'll end up unhappy. What if we don't have the right information to make the smartest choice? We may even feel as though we lack the confidence to be bold because we don't want to let anyone down. But never forget that God will lavish wisdom on us if we ask. He will counsel us in the right direction every time. And when we keep close to Him, we'll be brave and wise to choose with conviction.

Divine Benefits

Yahweh, you alone are my inheritance. You are my prize, my pleasure, and my portion. You hold my destiny and its timing in your hands. Your pleasant path leads me to pleasant places. I'm overwhelmed by the privileges that come with following you!

PSALM 16:5–6 TPT

Yes, there are privileges we receive when we choose to follow the Lord with our life. There are divine benefits that come from being a believer, and they can't be replicated anywhere else. While we shouldn't choose to follow Him for the goodie bag alone, there are countless good things faith brings. God Himself is a blessing we can't help but embrace. So if you're on the fence with faith today, uneasy or unsure about going all-in, let today's scripture encourage you to say *yes* to God's gift of salvation. You'll be overwhelmed by the privileges that come from following!

Prayers from a Place of Stress

*Don't dump me, GOD; my God, don't
stand me up. Hurry and help me; I want
some wide-open space in my life!*
PSALM 38:21-22 MSG

Sometimes we worry about what God is thinking because we've made a mess of our life. We've gone from bad choice to bad choice, and we feel certain we've pushed Him to the limit. Have you ever prayed like the psalmist, asking God to stick with you and not give up? It's a prayer prayed from a place of stress, and it's unnecessary. You don't have to beg the Lord to love you. You don't have to ask Him to stay in relationship with you. The reality is there is no circumstance that would ever make Him dump you. God won't ever stand you up. So let that fear fade, and replace it with His promise to never leave you.

What a Stress-Free Life Looks Like

Because of you, I know the path of life, as I taste the fullness of joy in your presence. At your right side I experience divine pleasures forevermore!
PSALM 16:11 TPT

This is what a stress-free life looks like. When God is in the driver's seat and we relinquish the control we desperately cling to, we'll find a life full of peace. Inviting the Lord to be part of each day allows us to be in His presence continually, and it blesses us. We'll find energy and motivation to walk the path He has chosen and planned. Rather than battle anxious thoughts, joy will fill our heart. And eternity will be our next breath in the end. Our only hope for a peace-filled life on earth is to stay in the presence of God.

Scripture Index

Proverbs

About the Author

Carey Scott is an author, speaker, and certified Biblical Life Coach who's honest about her walk with the Lord—stumbles, fumbles, and all. With authenticity and humor, she challenges women to be real, not perfect, and reminds them to trust God as their source above all else. Carey lives in Colorado with her two kids, who give her plenty of material for writing and speaking. She's surrounded by a wonderful family and group of friends who keep her motivated, real, and humble. You can find her at CareyScott.org.